MW01294122

0

The Enemy Within

Dealing with Fear

By Jim Banks

Other books by Jim Banks

The Effects of Trauma and How to Deal With It, 3rd Edition
A Workbook (for the above noted title)
Boundaries
Angels and Demons
One Calling, One Ministry
Choose Your Outcome (w/ Mandy Valdes)
Sex Trafficking Ministry Manual (w/ Becca Wineka)
Hope for Freedom
Just Thinking
Defeating Jezebel
Finding Your Life Calling
Helping Your Veteran Deal with the Effects of Trauma
Finishing Well
Cast A Long Shadow

All are available on Amazon.com

Copyright 2018 Jim Banks

All Rights Reserved

www.houseohealingministries.org

www.traumaprayer.com

email: office@houseofhealingministries.org

All scripture quotations, unless otherwise noted, are taken from the Holy Bible, Authorized King James Version, Public Domain, or from the Revised Standard Version of the Bible, copyright 1952 [2nd edition, 1971] by the Division of Christian Education of the National Council of the Churches of Christ in the United States of America. Scripture quotations marked (NKJV) are taken from the New King James Version. Copyright 1982, Thomas Nelson, used by permission. All Rights Reserved.

Please note that House of Healing Ministries publishing style capitalizes certain pronouns in Scripture that refer to the Father, Son, and Holy Spirit and may differ from some Bible publishers' style.

Please note that the name satan and any related names are purposely not capitalized. We choose not to acknowledge him even to the point of violating grammatical rules.

© Copyright 2018 – Jim Banks
All Rights Reserved. No part of this book may be reproduced in any form, except for the inclusions of brief quotations in review, without expressed written permission by the author/publisher.

Printed in the U.S.A.

About the Author

Jim Banks' formal training was in electrical engineering. He served as an electrical design engineer on industrial projects for several years with a consulting house in Houston, TX. Later he moved into design work modernizing the electrical infrastructure of older buildings to provide for the needs of modern electronic devices. This technical background allowed him to make a career move into sales and marketing where he worked for several industrial manufacturers, serving as sales and marketing manager for several firms. His wife, Pat, worked as an executive trainer for Southwestern Bell for many years. Together they have four children and six grandchildren. They entered the inner-healing ministry over thirty years ago, initially on a part-time basis, the last sixteen of which have been full-time,

Operating out of a local church, Jim and Pat established a healing community in Asheville, NC, in 2005. That community continues to offer a broad range of classes, support groups, individual sessions, and therapies which are able to help an individual walk through just about any situation where emotional and spiritual problems have created unresolved painful issues, broken relationships, and daily dysfunctionality.

Jim and Pat are the founders of House of Healing Ministries. Through their vision casting, teaching, and mentoring, they have helped establish dozens of healing centers and healing communities across the nation. They have trained over 7,000 people in some phase of physical and emotional healing in the last eight years alone.

They also travel extensively doing member care for a couple of US based foreign missionary agencies, working principally in Africa and Southeast Asia.

Their hearts' desire is to raise up numerous comprehensive, lay-led healing communities wrapped around one or more local congregations to serve their local community with the healing hand of Jesus. One of their efforts is to offer multiple events around the country, their "Inner Healing & Deliverance RoundTables and Symposiums," through which they introduce various inner healing and deliverance modalities and programs that contribute to a comprehensive healing community.

They also offer private personal prayer ministry by appointment.

The Enemy Within

Chapter One

Dealing With Fear

My wife (Pat) and I work in a sector of the mental health field that gets no play, not that we need it. We don't need a pat on the back, and we certainly don't need promoters because we have a whole world of potential customers who need to see us. We call ourselves prayer ministers because that's largely what we do. We typically limit our work to addressing the spiritual effects of trauma, wounding, abuse, rape, divorce, loss, death, abandonment, betrayal and rejection that has effectively crippled more people emotionally and physically than all the world's wars combined.

On occasion, the wrestling match over lost peace and contentment has tumbled over into territory that is normally considered to be under the purview of certified mental health professionals, but regardless of the presenting issues and how they originated, it invariably involved dealing with the dysfunctions and other unfortunate consequences caused by the client's inappropriate responses to various fears that wrested control of their lives from their hands and made off with the remnants of their horded emotional safety. Now I hope that you appreciate that I am trying to sum up that challenge a bit more eloquently than the usual stream of four letter words that people use in our office in an

10

attempt to describe how the frustration of the stuff they are struggling with makes them feel.

I have hesitated for as long as I could in addressing this issue in writing because it has such a wide range of symptoms and causes that the effort seemed to be nothing short of monumental. But in recent days I have run into so many people whose lives are literally being torn apart by it that I can no longer stand by and do nothing, for there is an answer. It's not like there isn't an absolute pile of books already out there that deal with one or more of the elements of fear, written by some amazing people who are much more qualified that I to speak to it, and it's not like I am the highly exalted grand poobah of experts on this subject sporting my own unique trademarked insights. However, that having been said .... I can assure you that in the last 30 years I've seen some stuff! And I hate what it has done to God's most prized creations.

To top it off, I don't think I have ever witnessed more people who have become totally incapacitation by anxiety and panic attacks, for seemingly no reason at all. Our good friend Mandy Valdes, who operates a Chic Fil-A restaurant in the north Atlanta, area just told us of his experience with two late teen girls who work for him being suddenly struck with debilitating anxiety out of nowhere as they walked through the dining room to begin their shifts. Each collapsing in his arms, in a puddle of tears saying, I don't know what's come over me? I don't know what's wrong!

I don't think I need to recount everything that is going on in the world today that is fostering fear on a daily basis, for it is obvious that scripture has accurately predicted precisely what we are experiencing;

> Matthew 24:6a *"And you shall hear of wars and rumors of wars: see that you be not troubled:"*

Luke 21:25-26 *"And there will be signs in the sun and moon and stars, and on the earth distress of nations in perplexity because of the roaring of the sea and the waves,*
26 people fainting with fear and with foreboding of what is coming on the world. For the powers of the heavens will be shaken."

The difficulty is that everyone around us is struggling with fear and as they do our whole environment has become increasingly saturated with it, which the enemy uses against us to try and leverage us into falling deeper into the iron grip of fear as well. Should we not be concerned about the events of our time, our nation and our city? Certainly we should be concerned, but concern and fear are not the same thing and you need to be certain which one you are waking in, for one of them is wisdom and the other is death. To be clear, concern is defined as: to relate to; be connected with; be of interest or importance, while fear is defined as: a distressing emotion aroused by impending danger, disaster, evil, pain, etc., whether the threat is real or imagined; the feeling or condition of being afraid. More on this later.

This past week or so has been interesting because I have received five emails from women who have listened to one of the versions of the Trauma Prayer (www.traumaprayer.com) that I have recorded over the past few years and they were able to report that they found comfort and some healing in it. These five have been married to abusers (physical and/or emotional) for close to two decades each and have come to the end of their individual ropes emotionally and were asking for help. Their cries for help come with the realization that the depth of their plight (misery) is partially their fault because they put up with it for so long thinking that it would get better. It is also founded in the fact that they had; a) given up their voice in the face of persistent abusive treatment (verbal, physical or sexual), b) refused to fight for personal respect of any kind in their marriage, c) or chose to live in faint hope that

12

one day he would come to his senses and begin treating them as a husband should. Instead, it has simply gotten worse. None of them think they can put up with it anymore. They have been worn down and finally lost hope for a change.

The bottom line is that they have given into fear and for very several understandable reasons. They feel imprisoned in the relationship for a myriad of reasons many of which are founded in some measure of truth, such as, not knowing if they can take care of themselves or their children financially if they leave the marriage. None have any visible means of support readily available (relationships) to help them because over time they and their abuser have isolated themselves in their misery and because each of them is in their forties and have been out of the workforce raising children they collectively feel like they are unemployable – hence they are trapped financially.

Then there is the loss of a preferable future. Because of their abusive marriages none of them are interested in marrying again. Even in that, there are a myriad of conflicting issues, such as; I'm still in love with the one who abused me, but I can't take it anymore. I have older kids to take of and who wants a woman with teenaged children to support? I didn't make a very good decision last time and I certainly don't want to make the same mistake again. I have no resources and don't want me and my kids to have to live in a shelter. And the biggie, I don't want to face the beating I'll get when he finds out I'm gone and he figures out where I went. All of which may have some validity, yet all are solidly based in fear.

As an aside; not being one who is in favor of divorce simply for the sake of the impact it has on children, my advice would be to: first, seek safety for yourself and your children, secondly, engage with law enforcement to deal with the abuser. And third, assuming you don't have family to turn to, engage with the local representatives of your state's welfare agencies to see what support and social services are available to you free of charge, including those of a lawyer. You and your children are entitled to live in peace without the continuing threat of violence. And who knows, perhaps leaving him will be the move that causes your husband to seek help. Yes, it is possible, but it still sounds pretty lame, but I've seen more amazing things than that.

The bottom line for these ladies is that because they have children with their abuser, they will be connected to him in some way for the remainder of their lives, and fairly closely while the children are adolescents. If you've been physically abused and threatened with your life, hanging around for more is a really scary thought. Yes, the court will tell you that you can get a restraining order put in place that will keep your abusing spouse away from you, but the only ones who can make sure that doesn't happen are members of local law enforcement, which is usually 10 to 20 minutes away, time enough for you to be beaten to death two or three times.

When we look at the actual bottom line here we find all throughout these marriages, including the review of reasons keeping them from leaving and the hurdles they'll have to jump through if they do choose to leave, there is the ever present specter of fear. It is not only the crappy decision that they blame for ushering them into the abusive situation in the first place that is fearful, but the fear of making another lousy decision in trying to correct the problem that could actually make it much worse than it is already. Usually, each of them has reached this decision point after having lived in this hell for years, they are worn out from the stress, the anxiety and the combination of spiritual, emotional and physical weariness. Consequently, their line of thinking is really messed up and if it's messed up, then there is good reason not to trust the next series of decisions.

Psalm 91:5-7a has a couple of verses in that sums up fear for us;

> *"You will not fear the terror of the night, nor the arrow that flies by day,*
> *nor the pestilence that stalks in darkness, nor the destruction that wastes at noonday.*
> *A thousand may fall at your side, ten thousand at your right hand,"*

The promise is that if we will snuggle up to God then we will not be driven into fear by the potentially hurtful things we can see with our eyes, nor the ones we can't see at night but know that they are out there waiting for us.

God has incessantly throughout his Word offered His sacred promised to protect us from harm. Psalm 91 is a perfect example of that promise. What we would like to assume is that if I snuggle up to the Lord all this nasty stuff will go away, or I won't see it and therefore won't have to deal with it. That's our narcissistic way of viewing things which has no connection to reality, for Jesus Himself said, *"In this world you are gonna have trouble, but don't get in fear over it, I've got this."* (my paraphrase) If you have lived life for any length of time at all you have realized that trouble will come like waves onto the beach, regularly, but not continuously. Fortunately, it's more like irregularly, but even that's too frequent for me. When you want to take God at His word and yet expect everything to go according to your preferred expectations as to what fulfillment of His promise looks like, disappointment is going to be your constant companion.

Why is that? Because Psalm 91 5-7 says you are going to see with your own eyes the arrows that fly by day, you are going to personally witness the destruction that happens in broad daylight. Not only that, but you are assured that you are going know that sheer terror, death and pestilence are raging outside your front door every night, and when you rise and head for the grocery store you will not be able to escape the images of the dead and dying on the side of the road all the way there.

Whoah! Is that literally what it's going to be like? Well, in reality there is always that possibility as long as there are deranged men and women on this planet, but neither is it totally metaphoric. The fact is you and I are bombarded by media every day with all the dreadful activities that occur every 5 minutes around the world somewhere. Two days ago there were eruptions of two volcanoes that killed at least 103 people, one in Guatemala and a minor one in Mexico. At the same time lava was still flowing relentlessly like a river from fissures around the base of a volcano in Hawaii that had thus far destroyed over 600 homes.

Deaths resulting from protesters clashing with police and army personnel continue to mount in Nicaragua. Approximately 32 people have died everyday in clashes in Syria for the last four years. Reports of school shootings, cop killings, and street violence in Chicago, Washington DC, New Orleans, etc. are in the news every day. Recently released statistics for murders in Venezuela topped 34,100 in 2017 and over the weekend of August 3-5, 74 people were shot in Chicago and 122 uncontrolled wild fires were burning in seven Western States. Then when you throw in rampant flooding, torrential rains from sub-tropical storms systems, tornadoes, drought, hurricanes, crop devastation from roaming herds of feral hogs in Texas, stock market volatility, several States unable to properly fund promised pension funds for teachers and state employees, stories of Social Security becoming bankrupt by 2020, North Korea's unstable leadership threatening to nuke whoever they don't like, South Africa's Cape Town running out of water due to government corruption and incompetence, Greece is remaining on the verge of bankruptcy, blah, blah, blah blah and it's no wonder we want to go hide somewhere.

If you choose to take the images of this passage in Psalm 91:5-7 metaphorically, do so, but don't ignore the images around you of the homeless, the people living under bridges and viaducts, the poor, the bag-ladies with shopping carts loaded with all their worldly possessions, the poor in the market who have to decide how to spend what little they have in order to feed their family. Were it not for the protection and provision of the Lord, one of these folks could be you.

Now I don't want to belabor the point but we live in a society where everybody seems to be mad about something, one where the phrase "going postal" has significant implications for us today, even as it did when that phrase was coined in 1986. The sad part of the drastic picture I have just painted for you is that all this is going on as I am writing this in mid 2018 and by the time you read it most of this will be 'old hat' and long forgotten, because it will have been supplanted by a whole new batch of bad news available for you to get concerned about, and the system of the world will be happy to bring it fresh to your door daily, even hourly if you would like – virtually free of charge. A lot of it may even be fake news just to mess up your day and keep you riled up about something or someone.

(Here's a stray thought I just had: If the media is becoming known for its fake news and publishing biased commentary as truth and now has the lowest confidence rating by news consumers in 35 years … and the devil (who hates us) was characterized by Jesus as "a liar and the father of lies … the truth is not in him" (John 8:44), then we would be correct in understanding that the media is his tool being used against us.

The hard part of it is that we would like to remain informed about what is going on in the world, just in case it impacts us personally, and we need to do something about it. (Consider the recent spate of contaminated food product recalls.) At the same time, we don't want it to intrude into our daily lives that we have been so diligently trying to keep safe and serene. However, fear is neither a respecter of your boundaries, nor your wishes. In fact, it has an agenda that guarantees that if you even covertly choose to peek under its covers, just out of innocent curiosity, you can say goodbye to your precious safety and serenity, for in so doing you will have encountered the specter of evil possibilities face-to-face.

If you will not master fear, it will master you.

Chapter Two

A Brief Summary

In the foregoing I have catalogued a number of specific fears that we collectively experience in life, some quite obvious, some less so. What follows in this book are a series of fears that are not only less obvious, but are disguised as something else and are consequently more difficult to identify. For many these fears would seem to be inconsequential, however for others, they can be the very thing which paralyzes them to the extent that their world seem unbearable, stopping them from not only enjoying the life they have but robbing them of a preferable future. When we boil it all down, here are what I believe to be the major contributing factors to the fear that we commonly experience today.

1. Higher order demonic entities over countries and over regions of the country whose mission is to instill fear in the inhabitants of that nation or region for the purpose of antagonizing them, driving them into anxiety, panic and depression and finally causing to despair of life itself.
2. Demonic deception that is rather like a veil pulled over the eyes of certain segments of the population that causes them to fear the actions of other segments of the population, which requires them to either viciously attack or throw rocks from a distance.

3. The performance orientation of the society we live in created by the system of the world (satan) and it mission to derail or permanently damage your individual God-given identity and purpose.
4. Your own dysfunctional iniquitous belief systems that are passed down by the members of your family or origin.
5. The lies and half-truths that you have come to believe through the mis-interpretation of life's circumstances and people's motives that came as a result of the losses, hurts and rejection that you have experienced which have created your current array of insecurities and self-protection mechanisms.

In the fight to deal with fear it is always best to deal with items one and two (above) first and in many cases the problem will be solved within minutes.

Ask God to deal with all the higher order demonic entities first, repenting for any personal agreement with them first, then asking forgiveness on behalf of any ancestors who agreed with them bringing assignments and curses upon you and the family line.

Secondly, ask forgiveness of the Lord for worrying about things real or imagined and attempting to control circumstances yourself. Ask forgiveness for being self-sufficient, self-willed and refusing to bow to His superiority in such matters. Break any place of agreement and any contracts you have made, either verbally or by your action or inaction, with the lower order demonic spirits of fear, worry, and anxiety. Tell them to leave immediately and give that ground back to the Lord Jesus Christ for Him to rule and reign over. Then give whatever the problem is to Jesus to work out at His pleasure, making certain that you do not complain in the aftermath.

Items three, four and five from above will be discussed later on in this writing and may well be the most difficult items to process through because they deal with how you think, the habit patterns you have created that lead to fear and the lies you believe about God's ability that have led you to try to control you circumstances which have become overwhelming.

Trust in God is a very hard thing to re-establish because we typically look to our circumstance as that which provides validity and veracity for our beliefs rather than to the truth of the Word of God. We want what we want now and when He doesn't show up on our time table we get disappointed and throw our miniscule faith overboard and partner again with fear, this time more deeply.

Fear has a number of goals, however its primary one is to isolate you, to get you to retreat into your own world to think your own dark thoughts, to separate you from all life giving relationships, to cause you to feel so miserable and hopeless that you will eventually take you own life. Whether it is successful in achieving that goal or not is immaterial, for in the process you will become the person most unlike your true self. No matter how great your fears are you always have a choice, even if it doesn't seem like it. You don't have to live with it. You have a choice. Break agreement with it and you will find that God is there to help you walk free of it.

I believe it was Derik Prince who said that, *"God will deliver you from your enemies, but He will not deliver you from your friends."*

The first steps in dealing with fear is talking about it.

Chapter Three

The Bigger Picture

This next topic actually goes without saying, but just for the record, there is a much larger contest going on here than just what you are dealing with; the ultimate cosmic conflict between good and evil, between God and satan, and like it or not, you and I are part of this contest.

For the record, you were created by God. There is a video on the home page of our website www.houseofhealingministries.org that gives the background of this story that you may want to hear. Now, with all that I have written and recorded that spoke about and to the uniqueness of your creation, which I shall not replicate here, it is also my guess that there was another party there that was a witness to all of God's magnificent creative display the day you were made … Lucifer. He was probably there applauding each and every exquisite choice The Father made as He lovingly fashioned you for His purposes, silently taking note of everything Father did – even the *"vessels made for honor and dis-honor."* (Romans 9:21)

Sometime later, Lucifer began to think that he should at the least be on the same level as, or perhaps even *higher than God …*

> *Ezekiel 28:14-17 "Thou art the anointed cherub that covereth; and I have set thee so: thou wast upon the holy mountain of God; thou hast walked up and down in the*

midst of the stones of fire. 15 Thou wast perfect in thy ways from the day that thou wast created, till iniquity was found in thee. 16 By the multitude of thy merchandise they have filled the midst of thee with violence, and thou hast sinned: therefore I will cast thee as profane out of the mountain of God: and I will destroy thee, O covering cherub, from the midst of the stones of fire. 17 Thine heart was lifted up because of thy beauty, thou hast corrupted thy wisdom by reason of thy brightness: I will cast thee to the ground, I will lay thee before kings, that they may behold thee."

... and there was a war in Heaven. Lucifer lost, and the sentence for his thoughts and actions was pronounced by God;

Ezekiel 28:18-19 "Thou hast defiled thy sanctuaries by the multitude of thine iniquities, by the iniquity of thy traffic; therefore will I bring forth a fire from the midst of thee, it shall devour thee, and I will bring thee to ashes upon the earth in the sight of all them that behold thee. 19 All they that know thee among the people shall be astonished at thee: thou shalt be a terror, and never shalt thou be any more."

Even though the above verses speak of his ultimate demise, in the short term Lucifer got his butt kicked, and he and his whole rebellious crew were booted out of Heaven: *"And he (Jesus) said unto them, I beheld satan as lightning fall from heaven."* (Luke 10:18)

Revelations 12:7-9 "And there was war in heaven: Michael and his angels fought against the dragon; and the dragon fought and his angels, 8 And prevailed not; neither was their place found any more in heaven. 9 And the great dragon was cast out, that old serpent, called the Devil, and

> Satan, **which deceiveth the whole world:** he was cast out
> into the earth, and his angels were cast out with him."

> Isaiah 14:12-14 *"How art thou fallen from heaven, O*
> *Lucifer, son of the morning! how art thou cut down to the*
> *ground, which didst weaken the nations! 13 For thou hast*
> *said in thine heart, I will ascend into heaven, I will exalt my*
> *throne above the stars of God: I will sit also upon the*
> *mount of the congregation, in the sides of the north: 14 I*
> *will ascend above the heights of the clouds; I will be like the*
> *most High."*

I think it is interesting to note that our God is always merciful, even
as he was merciful to Lucifer by not obliterating him as an entity
from the universe. God knows, there are many of us who from time
to time would love to have that job ourselves if we could, but since
He even prizes the jerks we come in contact with, He's reserved
that judgment for Himself.

Unfortunately for us, God didn't annihilate him, so his high impact
face plant destination was the earth where he became known as:

> *"Wherein in time past ye walked according to the course of*
> *this world, according to the* **prince of the power of the air,**
> *the spirit that now works in the children of disobedience."*
> (Ephesians 2:2).

The war between he (now known as the devil or satan) and God
continues to this day.

Once Lucifer was "shown the door," make that, "given the left foot
of fellowship," and found himself doing a serious face-plant on
planet earth, he was really mad! Mad at God, mad at where he
found himself, mad at his demotion, mad that he lost the war, mad

at what he saw when he arrived (dinosaurs and the like) and eventually mad at man when he showed up! As the new king of this domain he immediately set about to show God a thing or two about His prized possessions, His creation and the people He fashioned for Himself for "His good pleasure!"

That is how you and I came to be involved in this overarching cosmic war between God and satan. It is why bad things happen to good people. It is why there are wars, murders, rapists, robbers, politicians, lawyers, thieves, crappy government and ultimately why there are so many bad decisions made by people that result in loss, death and destruction for the rest of us. It is also the reason why we have so many laws.

So he (the devil, satan, the former Lucifer) tricked Adam and Eve, the first man and woman sent to earth to rectify (redeem) the damage (John 10:10) that Lucifer had done when he was sentenced to earth. He snookered Adam and Eve into turning over to him authority over the earth that they had received in Genesis 1:26-28 while still in the Garden of Eden. Through that broken and sinful pair, God established a race of people to call His own and through them brought the 2nd Adam (Jesus), the first a natural son of man, the second a spiritual son, to redeem both earth and man. (1 Corinthians 15:46)

It is God's specific plan to restore to man the power to do what the first Adam could not get done, bring the rule and reign of God the Father over the entire earth through His children, mankind.

Now in his wrath, satan knew how each of us was created and probably what we were created for because (it is my thought that) he was one of the original witnesses to our individual creation.

(Sometimes you can tell a great deal about a person's destiny by simply identifying where and how they have been attacked over their lifetime.) So that was what he went after – our personal identity and purpose. If you don't know who you are and why you are here, anything and everything is an option for you. That's similar to the old saying, *"If you don't know where you're going, any road will take you there."* Most of us know the pain of winding up in a place we had no business being, and the arduous task of getting back on course.

So satan's attack is launched against who you are – your identity. He doesn't need to assign a horde of demons to your case to keep you messed up. He started with your ancestors getting them to fall into all sorts of sin and entanglements. They built numerous mental ideologies and structures of thoughts about why things are the way they are (called their truth) and why stuff happens. They dutifully taught them to their children, so in time they eventually became your truth, even if it has no resemblance to the real truth or the reality of life at all.

These things are called iniquitous family patterns, or belief systems; things like how you treat women and children; how you think about other races; thought process about poverty and material possessions; how you think about wealth and those who have it or don't, including how to get it; what are acceptable public and private expressions of anger and how to treat people that offend you. This even includes political party affiliations. These are the things get passed on from generation to generation. They are not necessarily intentionally taught, just caught.

Many of their behaviors also bring on curses and demonic attachments. The curses are reinforced by each successive generation and the demonic attachments grew stronger with each passing generation that falls into the same sin as their predecessors.

Then there were the direct assaults against your personhood, when you were at your weakest and most vulnerable. These included vicious wounds like the death of a parent(s), divorce, abandonment, sexual molestation, rape, sodomy, rejection, being given up for adoption, poverty, mental and physical abuse, emotional and physical abandonment, or having had to grow up with parents who were drug or alcohol addicted, or who were rage-alcoholics.

In response to the pain of each event we built walls out of fear of experiencing further hurt and pain. They in turn kept out everything, including the love we so desperately desired; more trauma occurred and the enemy was there to feed us more lies about ourselves.

For so many it meant living a life with no high or lows because significant portions of our heart was shut down years ago because of the fear of the possibility of experiencing more pain. Simply existing is no fun whatsoever for there is no 'real' life there. After a few years it's hard to even say that it is better than what you had that you are so fearful of. Yes, there's no daily or weekly pain now, but there's no joy either. The best you can say is that at least it's predictable.

Over time you find yourself in a place of isolation and disconnection, with a heart that is shut down and cold as a stone. You yearn for real life, but everything seems to be a poor imitation of it. The enemy has you right where he wants. You've lost touch with who you are, or you've failed to develop your own identity because you have hidden it for most of your life fearing that no one would like you if they really knew you. Since you have no clue who you really are, and have no idea why you're here, there is no corresponding sense of destiny, or purpose. Hence there is no personal vision, no passion and no opportunity for fulfillment.

We have all been there on one level or another. To those who have been horrifically abused and traumatized, is feels like a lifetime and there appears to be no hope for a come-back.

Then there are the spiritual attacks against our emotional, spiritual and relational progress. The enemy doesn't like it at all when you are beginning to mature and do things like forgiving offences and determining not to judge each other, growing close with other believers and spending time with family. Nor can he allow you to accidentally get close to following your dreams. John 10:10a says,

> "The thief cometh not, but for to steal, and to kill, and to destroy:"

which is another way of saying,

> "...In the world ye shall have tribulation:" (John 16:33)

But there's good news. Jesus said in,

> John 10:10b "I am come that you might have life, and that they might have it more abundantly."

When Jesus appeared on the scene, in whom was all the fullness of God Himself, He firmly established the fact that there was a new Sheriff in town! He went about deputizing (giving power and authority to) all who would follow him. To those Deputies He gave the 'dunamis' power of the Holy Spirit to kick spiritual butt and take names; to break the power of sin (generational and otherwise) off man, to break the power of the defilement of sin off the land

and set it free to be a blessing to man, and to re-establish Kingdom order in the house!

So now you know why the enemy's after your personal identity and why there is so much fear at work everywhere you go, for as God wrote in Revelations 12:7-9, "... *called the Devil, and Satan, **which deceiveth the whole world:*** " **this is the only weapon he's got left.**

The good news is ... as hard as this seems to be on us, God has a plan and He's not concerned about achieving His heart's purposes at all. He has secretly been preparing a mighty army of folks who have been through hell and have survived to help others. These folks may or may not be in a church. Some of them still are. But they have a couple of things in common; they love God, and they love people in a practical manner that requires them to give of themselves, and they now have some effective weapons to use gathered during their trip through hell. All in all, a magnificent fulfillment of Matthew 22:37-40.

The good news is that these folks are gathering together to form healing communities of varying sizes and descriptions; from a few folks who get together once a week to pray for the sick, to dozens who meet all over the city doing inner healing, deliverance, working with the abused, drug addicted, the abandoned, the sexually and relationally broken, the widows and the orphans, the prisons, half-way houses and shelters all across America and in foreign countries you'll never visit.

My wife and I have been extremely privileged these last few years to be able to travel and help establish some of them and then to nourish several others all across the southern US. It's fun to watch God do His thing and meet the special people who have answered His call.

What we have attempted to impart is a few of the tools God has taught us that will help an individual re-establish his/her personal identity. Somewhere in the process we can give them a few ideas that will allow God to assist them to recover lost and stolen dreams and visions for their lives, then given them some guidance in how to practically express it.

This is especially true for folks like artists and musicians. There is an old joke running around that asks the question, "How can a musician (artist) end up with a million dollars? Answer: Start with two million." What we have historically known is that this group of people are often referred to as "starving artists." The fact remains that if that's the driving force that God gave you, then there exists a means by which it can be satisfied and you can be fulfilled (and provided for) in the process. Yes, there is a training period and seasoning required to find your voice and your singular means of expression, along with sufficient skill, professionality and experience to carry it. Until you find/develop it your peak earning years will still be ahead of you, but that still doesn't mean that you will have to starve in the meantime. Remember, all the promises of provision detailed in Matthew 6 were written specifically for you.

> Psalm 37:25 *"I have been young and I am now old, yet I have not seen the righteous abandoned, nor his children begging bread."*

There are a couple of other books I have written that cover dealing with the demonic that would be helpful for you to get for there are times when that is the only answer to the problem. They are *Angels and Demons, Knowing What You're Up Against* and *Defeating Jezebel*. The latter is our personal story of how we were taught to deal with the enemy that got us out of a very common hole that many people find themselves in. Both of them are available at

Amazon.com and I hope you you'll take advantage of the wisdom provided by learning from our mistakes and the story of our restoration through Jesus Christ.

Chapter Four

Another Source of Fear, Natural Disasters

One of the biggest issues with fear is the development of the presence of fear that is inculcated, woven into the fabric of our culture through fear-based mindsets that rule our decision making processes. It is in the very foundation of almost everything we have been taught.

You and I were created in the image of God, who according to scripture is love. (1John 4:8) Scripture also informs us that *"there is no fear in love, for perfect love casts out fear."* (1John 4:18) Consequently, I can say without fear of contradiction that you and I were not made either 'for fear', or 'to fear', we were taught it. If we were taught it, then certainly we can 'un-learn' it. Jesus said. *"If you love me, you will keep my commandments."* He also commanded this,

> *"I have said these things to you, that in me you may have peace. In the world you will have tribulation. But take heart (have no fear); I have overcome the world." (John 16:33)*

It is obvious that bad things happen in this world that will impact us, most of which are far beyond our control: natural disasters, flood, fires, hurricanes, abuse, betrayals, financial depressions, wars, business failures, cancer, relational disasters, abuse, deaths, robbery, auto accidents that maim and cripple, etc. When we respond in fear, we will never get to one that overcame the affects of the world – we simply wallow in them. We do have another choice.

Even the Apostle Paul who wrote much of the New Testament experienced it,

> 2Corinthians 1:8-9a *"For we do not want you to be unaware, brothers, of the affliction we experienced in Asia. For we were so utterly burdened beyond our strength that we despaired of life itself. 9 Indeed, we felt that we had received the sentence of death."* (ESV)

If we know intellectually that we will be tempted to respond in fear, why do we continually go immediately to fear? It is because the 'things' we lose during these "tribulations" (troubles), whether they are single events, or consistent over a period of time, directly conflict with our established personal value system and sense of personal security, especially so here in America.

Remember the phrase, *"If I do right, everything will be right?"* Our fear is rooted in our personal sense of right and wrong, as well as a view of the way things should work in a logical, orderly, well tuned society – it creates and sustains our sense of security. Those elements of proper order anchor our view of what will provide and maintain our personal security and sense of peace … if we always "do right." Our expectation is that if you put a coin (our performance) in the slot (of the system of the world) that it should properly deliver to us peace, joy and economic stability every time, as though it was a machine.

Our horror at a disaster's violation of the things we value signal to us that our losses are actually a failure in our own personal responsibility, along with providing a statement of our personal worth. Surely we could have anticipated this, or done something more to protect ourselves against these losses! I could have done something more to prevent it, or at least mitigate it. I should have seen it coming and been better prepared.

Fundamentally, the greatest reason we go immediately to fear is that we value the wrong things. Those misplaced values dictate our priorities in life and create the earnest expectation that they should be protected at all costs, and especially by God. Consequently, it is no wonder our peace and tranquility immediately evaporates when they are threatened or lost.

Further, if our personal value as a human being is established and maintained by either the material possessions we acquire, or the favor in life we receive is seen as the system's payment for doing things right, then the foundation of our self-esteem is built on a very fragile footing. One brief, but strong wind of adversity could strip us of it all, and a 2 Corinthians 1:8-9 sized natural disaster could absolutely crush us.

> Psalms 23:4 *"Yea, though I walk through the valley of the shadow of death, I will fear no evil: for thou art with me; thy rod and thy staff they comfort me." (KJV)*

I have an acquaintance out in the Western US who is a Christian that experienced a significant loss. She and 349 other families around her lost everything in the Waldo Canyon fire in the Summer of 2012. She reported that the devastation they experienced following the total loss of everything they owned was not only traumatic, but the grief brought on by losing all their family photos, cars, prized family heirlooms, personal memorabilia, etc, was virtually overwhelming for her and many of her friends. All that they loved and everything else they had worked for 30 years to acquire had been cruelly stripped from them in a matter of a few short minutes.

The devastation was so significant that she was at a complete loss in the next couple of weeks following the fire to do the simple practical things of recovery like buying underwear, replacing her medications, her glasses and getting a new phone, which she had mistakenly left behind in the rush to evacuate. For the next four months she lived in an all consuming fog of bereavement as though she had lost absolutely everything that meant anything to her, including all her family and friends. She said that she felt that her entire life had gone up in smoke that day.

This is a very typical response because to be sure, life is not only not the same anymore, but it will never be the same again for her or her neighbors. Trauma of this magnitude introduces several things everyone that experiences it has to personally resolve,

1) the loss of personal security, because the old normal has been destroyed, nothing appears to be the same, that which you unconsciously counted on to never change is gone and unavailable to you (your comfy bed, the grocery store, the cleaners, the personal records, the second vehicle, the trees and flowers you planted and sweated over for years, that favorite pair of shoes that were too ugly to wear in public but have become too comfortable to throw away) and the results of all the million little decisions you have made over the years (that you have forgotten about) now have to be made again. To be sure your old life is gone and can never be recovered.

2) the loss ushers in an uncertainty of the future, which is now a harsh reality, whereas before it was only a distant potential which could easily be held at arm's length, or totally dismissed at will.

3) In the case of major natural disasters, various government agencies from God-knows-where are now running the show in your community and you can no longer do what you want to, when you want to. Access to goods and services that you used to take for granted are now either unavailable or being rationed. This is also disconcerting because it signifies and cements that the loss has also brought a total lack of control over anything.

4) Then there is the aspect of abrupt change of life. What was once the mundane issues connecting us with work, shuttling kids to activities, church, doctor visits and grocery shopping, are now suddenly erased and the sole issue is immediate **survival**. The sudden evacuation itself made finding a temporary roof over your family's head a difficulty.

5) Here's probably the biggest hurdle of all. When someone loses everything they own as result of disaster, whether it at the hands of a fire, a flood, a hurricane, or an earthquake, they feel as though they have lost a part of themselves, and yet that feeling is hidden by the four other things noted above. The sense that they are no longer "whole and feel very vulnerable" brings a level of palpable emotional pain. They feel it and yet cannot recognize it for what it is, at least until some degree of "normalcy" is once again established and the beginnings of a routine are in place. For many this may take up to a year.

6) Then there's the palpable sense of grief and pain brought on by the magnitude of the loss. In a very real sense, you feel like you have lost a loved one, even if it was an inanimate object because you are still emotionally connected to that which no longer exists.

Any single one of these issues is fully capable of generating fear, but throw them all in the same pot and the porridge is overwhelming, no matter who you are. And it is all made that much more difficult to navigate because all the people in your support group (your friends) are going through the same thing at the same time and are of no support to you.

I don't want to minimize what she and her neighbors experienced because we naturally create emotional attachments to things that have meaning for us, such as our child's favorite stuffed animal that we have hung onto for 20 years; the animal was special to our child and therefore it became special to us. We generate attachments to homes, property and the area because it was the places where fond memories were created; a geographical location signifying belonging and one that defined your life. When those things are gone, they don't take the memories with them, but the physical means of attachment to the memories that have deep meaning has vanished. These are the things that life is made of and it is important for us to be able to have those devices that connect us to the memories of that season of life.

The loss is even made more tangible when, in the case of this woman, all she could now hold in her hand after the fire were the ashes and bits of melted glass and metal.

I am sure that their experience with this fire was horrific on many other levels as well, but what hit me was the reason she contacted me was that she wanted my advice on writing a book. She wanted to write a book for Christians on how to survive after your home burns to the ground, or some other natural disaster takes everything from you. I am certainly glad that she finally came out from under the fog she was consumed by to start processing the meaning of the event and initiate thinking about other people, however, winning the battle of recovery following a major economic loss also includes resetting your values so that you are not destroyed along with your possessions if it should happen to you again. You have to focus on what is really important, not what was important.

As I was in the final stages of writing this book the Carr Fire, in Redding, CA which as of August 8th) had destroyed 1,077 residences, 22 commercial structures, 500 outbuildings was in full fury. The fire was still ravaging thousands of acres a day, and at that point it had burned over 173,522 acres, and was only 47% contained. Of the 97,000 residents of the city of Redding, approximately 10% of the population became homeless in three days. Rental prices skyrocketed as some owners were trying to cash in on insurance money available to those who suffered the loss of everything. The enormity of this tragedy was widely covered by national news organizations on network TV, and only a few who lost everything were able to express their plight in a single recorded sound bite, which was only the tip-top of the iceberg of emotion that residents were experiencing.

I stumbled across a re-post of a brief composition by a victim of that fire which really put this whole thing in perspective for me.

I was struck by the Facebook Posts of Tony Stultzfus and his wife Kathy in the early days of August 2018, a week or so after the fire took their home, and have replicated them here for you because they portray both the difficulty of losing everything, including all your business/ministry resources, and well documents the healthy manner in which they are responding to this great tribulation.

Now ... understand that knowing how to respond is totally different that actually having to respond. Unless you have begun to address your values and fears now, the struggle to do so following an event like this will be monumental for you. However, thinking about it is not experiencing it.

Personal update on the Carr Fire

By Tony Stoltzfus, Redding, CA August 3, 2018

Well, that ends two adrenalin-fueled days of scurrying around like a chicken with my head cut off trying to find a house to rent. Calls to different rental agencies, insurance agent, claims people, homeowners, seeing several houses, and so many texts and messages and e-mails to respond to. If you sent me something and haven't gotten a reply, don't stop! Receiving so much love and support has kept me going. But I've done more texting in the last week than in the last 3 months, and more facebooking than in the last three years! I'll get there.

The biggest challenge today other than all the paperwork is that Kathy and me are in such different places in dealing with this. I had 5 days here right after the fire where I couldn't do anything except absorb it all--there was nothing I COULD do. Kathy came back two days ago after caring for her elderly mother for a week and fell right into a whirlwind of decisions and action steps. After snapping at each other all morning (and me losing my cool) I realized Kathy needs some time to absorb all this--she needs what I had while she was gone and I was staring at the wall and fire-watching. So she is off duty for the next few days and I am going to handle things. Someone sent us a nice gift of some cash, and I told her to go pamper herself with it this weekend.

I've gotten through what I am now calling my "zombie phase" (thinking slow, forgetting things, crying, not wanting to do anything, just absorbing all the prayers and expressions of love and support I got). In just two days I watched an entire season of one of my favorite shows (The Good Place), and even slept through a couple of them. Now I am ready to work.

Funny things keep happening. We are finalizing renting a house, and we spent a couple hours with the couple who own it so they are familiar with our situation. We were talking about utilities, and he said, "We have internet but not cable, but I could leave an apple TV here so you could watch Netflix." And I said, "Don't worry about it--we have a Roku we can use." He laughed at me, and all the sudden I realized, 'we USED to have a Roku. Now it's gone.' Your old life is still so real in your head, it just isn't there any more in the physical world.

We keep thinking of things we didn't realize are gone. That beautiful five-foot-high 'Praying Hands' painting we use in Transforming the Heart is gone. All Kathy's journals and all of my pre-computer ones are gone. We discovered we'd left two full boxes of uninsured audio CDs (part of our inventory) in a closet. Even the music we use in our Taste of Heaven is gone--we had to contact our Affiliate in Canada and have him (Chris Frost) send back a copy of our own music so we have it for our August workshop.

And every so often you see something that triggers you. We walked into the doctor's office this morning and the waiting room was furnished with beautiful, solid cherry Stickley mission-style chairs, a lot like the ones we built with our own hands (Kathy helped) and sat on for 25 years. We weren't quite ready for that.

But life goes on. We will have a nice, furnished house to stay in a week and a half, and a chance to catch our breath. Right now rebuilding just seems too painful, but we are going to wait a couple months to make that decision.

Alright -- gotta go see "Mission Impossible1"

Certainty, Suffering, and a Good God - Personal Update

By Tony Stoltzfus, Redding, CA Aug 4, 2014

Well, we rented a house so we have a place to stay for the next 6 to 12 months until we figure out what we are going to do. We can either rebuild or decide to take the insurance settlement and buy or build elsewhere. Right now, the idea of going back to our plot of land is hard to think about. All I can envision is the ashes, and that feels sad and painful. And overseeing the rebuilding of a whole house seems exhausting. It isn't just the structure—all the flowers and fruit trees and plants that we love would have to be replaced, and it would be years until they would really grow back.

So we are going to put off that decision. In a month or two, who knows how we will feel?

There is a craving for certainty you experience in the middle of all this chaos. Certainty means security; security means I can relax, I can think clearly, I'm okay. One of our friends offered us a place to rent a week ago and was willing to hold off on renting it and keep us first in line for it. Since the rental market here is going crazy, that was a huge gift! Just knowing we had an option, even if it wasn't perfect, (it) reduced our stress and let us think rationally about what to do. If we hadn't had an option, I'd have been sorely tempted to take the first place we looked at, and settled for much less than what we ended up getting.

We seek certainty in a lot of different ways in a crisis. Just having your car is certainty: there is at least one thing that is mine, that I can depend on having and using tomorrow. Every little thing we own can be a source of certainty, that we rely on to keep us secure.

Another way I can seek certainty in crisis or suffering is asking, "Why?" If I know the reason why I am suffering, I can do something about it—I can make a plan to protect myself from experiencing that pain in the future. If I can blame someone or something for my plight, I also get certainty. Then I am not the guilty one: I can be certain I didn't do this to myself.

Every so often the questions come up about how I responded in the crisis. Did I take the right things? (No—I'd take some totally different stuff if this happened again). Should I have turned on the sprinklers and left them on? (Maybe—I didn't want the firefighters to have no water when they needed it, but that may have been an irrelevant consideration). And how could I have forgotten to turn off the gas when I left? (That was a bit bone-headed!)

If I beat myself up over what I did, it is actually because I am looking for certainty. As humans, we cause ourselves pain to make sure we don't forget—so that the pain will ensure we remember to do the right thing next time. We beat ourselves up to protect ourselves from something we fear will be worse.

Sometimes I do the opposite—I try to reassure myself that I did the best I could under the circumstances, and that I am not the one to blame. It's the opposite of beating myself up, but I actually do it for basically the same reason: certainty. If I am not to blame, then I will not be punished, and I am not causing this to happen to myself. If I know that, I am in control, and I can feel certain and secure.

There are many things I could have done differently. What if I had made a list of what to take in a fire, and prepared for it beforehand? What if I had finished expanding our defensible space like I was planning? What if I had pressed my neighbors more to keep up their defensible space? There are no answers to those questions.

And I haven't wasted much time asking them. My certainty is not in being able to protect myself from pain, but that Jesus is with me in pain. I don't need to protect myself, because the best parts of me-- the greatest revelations, the deepest incarnation of Jesus in me, my dearest intimacies with Him—have all been birthed out of suffering. Suffering is not something to flee, but to embrace. I don't need to try to somehow manufacture suffering for myself to be holy (life will give me plenty of it without me even trying!), but I don't need to run away from it either. Suffering is not evidence of a breakdown in the goodness of God, but the place where the goodness of God is most evident.

One of the things that saddens me in this is how many people's instinctive response to my pain is to pray that I will get my stuff back, or even that God will give me more stuff than I had before. Their heart is to demonstrate the goodness of God, and I receive that heart and I am blessed by it. But I wonder: what is missing in us that our instinctive response to suffering is to try to get out of it, rather than meet Jesus in it? Have we forgotten the promises of God about suffering, and replaced them with a human promise of a pain-free life (that is found nowhere in the New Testament)? Have we lost sight of the fact that our lives are supposed to look like Jesus'?

Peter says that, "Since therefore Christ suffered in the flesh, arm yourselves with the same thought, for whoever has suffered in the flesh has ceased from sin, so as to live for the rest of the time in the flesh no longer by human passions but by the will of God." If you suffer, sinful desires no longer have a hold on you for the rest of your life?!? Dang, I'd suffer for that promise—wouldn't you?

Or how about this one: "When we cry, "Abba! Father!" it is the Spirit himself bearing witness with our spirit that we are children of

God, and if children, then heirs, heirs of God and fellow heirs with Christ, provided we suffer with him in order that we may also be glorified with him." Our cry of "Abba Father," our inheritance as children of God, is intrinsically linked to suffering with him in order that we might be glorified with him. I'd lose my house and never need to have it back for that!

Hebrews describes Jesus as the one whose suffering delivers those who "through fear of death are subject to lifelong bondage." For those who are afraid of suffering, deliverance from fear comes by one who passes through suffering, not one who skates around it. And we are to be like him. I know from repeated experience of loss, betrayal, want, and pain that the fear of suffering is not conquered by a God who promises I will never suffer, but a God who promises to be with me in it. Because he is with me, I don't have much fear of the one who can kill my body but cannot kill my soul. I only fear my God, who can destroy both soul and body in hell—or bring life to both in heaven.

Fear is not conquered through seeking certainty. It is not conquered by believing a Good God would never allow me to suffer. I triumph over suffering because I know Jesus can heal me of anything, not because I think he will protect me from everything. I know the one who is with me in whatever loss or grief I experience. He is good to me in whatever may come, he is sovereign enough to make so much beauty out of my ashes that I will have no regrets, and just being his is enough that I can face anything."

Thank you, Tony.

The personal recovery process will seemingly be as slow as the recovery of all the needful things you have lost, just make sure that the fear of losing it all again doesn't compound the loss you have just suffered.

Jesus spoke to this as well when He said, "*Whoever loves his life (and his stuff) loses it, and whoever hates his life in this world will keep it for eternal life.* (John 12:25) Understand that He's not talking about hating ourselves or our stuff. He is saying that when our value system exalts anything other than those things which Jesus imputes value to, it means that we are in love with those things, rather than life. We can measure it by the magnitude of despair, lack of peace, anger and sense of emptiness and the loss of security we are left feeling when those things are gone.

You need to know where you are getting your personal sense of value and security from for it is the secret to avoiding fear. If it is from your stuff, you are in big trouble.

Chapter Five

Another Expression of Fear

Let me give you another view of the impact that our estimate of our personal value and capabilities has on our decisions, and ultimately on potentially fulfilling our purpose. This one pertains to the view that we have of ourselves and consequently our ability. This is a piece of my story.

Back in the 90's I was invited to go to a men's retreat in Orlando, Florida. As I recall there were a little over 140 men in attendance from various churches all over the country. I don't remember much about the facility we were in but I do remember this snippet of the event as though it were this morning.

There was a breakout session held in another room which was approximately 1,400 square feet in size. The walls of the room were constructed of common cement blocks that you've seen 1,000 times, painted a pale blue color. The ceiling was a non-descript 2'x4' drop ceiling with 2'x'4 drop-in fluorescent light fixtures. To complete the poor acoustics, the flooring was the ubiquitous cream colored VCT, 10" square tile. And of course, the seating was your typical metal gray folding chairs – the ones with the thin one-hour (max) padding in them. As I recall, there were about 40 men assembled for this session.

The speaker was (I believe) at the time an Adjunct Professor of Evangelism from Fuller Theological Seminary in Pasadena, CA by the name of Ed Silvoso. He was in the middle of leading a series of trips to various cities in Argentina in an effort to show Americans how to win a city to Jesus in 30 days. The procedure was simple: divide the city up into manageable chunks on a map, assign people to cover each sector, connect with a local church in that sector and begin going door-to-door throughout the entire city simply asking people, "What is your greatest need that only God can take of? I want to pray for it to be supplied by Him." They would write down the address, a name and the need(s), and move on to the next house. Sometimes people would ask them to pray right then. Following their daily tour of interviews they would assemble in the evening and pray for these needs for a few hours.

In one week or so, they would visit these same homes again to see if there had been any progress. Invariably, there would be the joy of answered prayer for many individuals and families, and as time progressed more and more people would recognize God's hand moving not only in their own household, but on a widespread basis in their community.

And then it happened. In the midst of his presentation the speaker said, "*And this is how you pastor an entire city!*" In accord with my Baptist background, I was sitting about five or six rows from the back of the room among about a half-dozen other men, with a couple of chairs between each of us. I was leaning forward with my elbows on my knees looking down at some notes when he uttered those words. As he did the Holy Spirit hit me so hard in the abdomen that I flew backward into the row of chairs behind me, the unmistakable noise of the clattering of metal chairs on the hard floor surface reverberating throughout the room.

Flat on my back looking up to the ceiling, a vision suddenly appeared. It was a giant map of a major metropolitan city. I knew that city to be Atlanta, Georgia because that's where I was living at the time, an area of roughly 5.25 million people encompassing thirteen counties. The map was incredibly detailed. Every major highway, interstate, two lane road, neighborhood street and alley was there, along with railroad tracks, ponds, streams, rivers and lakes. And every detail was in crisp, clean brilliant color.

Immediately, I realized the connection of the map to the words just spoken – the implication was unmistakable – how YOU pastor a city! My thought was No, that's too big. As soon as that thought (fear) appeared, the map began to shrink. Immediately I realized what I had done and said, Stop! It stopped shrinking, but by that time it was perhaps only 60% of what it originally appeared to be. The conference ended and I returned to Atlanta not only stirred by what had happened, but wondering what to do with what I had experienced.

As I sat listening to the Lord sometime afterward, recording what I felt I had heard Him say, this spilled onto paper;

> *"You related to that vision but you couldn't see yourself over that much territory. So you shrank back from it. I wasn't pleased with your response because somehow you still relate it to personal responsibility. Your mind will tell you that it is not by your might or power, but by my Spirit that things get done. Yet your heart of hearts still chose to shrink back choosing to think that the assignment is too large for you and you'll be a failure.*
>
> *I am about to do heart surgery on you so that doesn't happen again. You have to learn that when I show you*

something like that map, I am saying, "This is what I want to do! Do you want to do it with me?"

Now I mentioned this event in my life because the presence of the fear of failure leads us to make some really poor decisions in life. Had I understood what the Lord was asking, I believe, or perhaps I hope, that I would have made a different choice. Do not let fear dictate the path of your life, for it will lie to you about what can be accomplished.

Here's another way to express it all from Shakespeare's view of fear recorded in his play Hamlet, 1603, in a modern language version:

> *" After all, who would put up with all life's humiliations—the abuse from superiors, the insults of arrogant men, the pangs of unrequited love, the inefficiency of the legal system, the rudeness of people in office, and the mistreatment good people have to take from bad—when you could simply take out your knife and call it quits? Who would choose to grunt and sweat through an exhausting life, unless they were afraid of something dreadful after death, the undiscovered country from which no visitor returns, which we wonder about without getting any answers from and which makes us stick to the evils we know rather than rush off to seek the ones we don't? **Fear of death makes us all cowards,** and our natural boldness becomes weak with too much thinking. Actions that should be carried out at once get misdirected, and stop being actions at all."*

We humans are intimately familiar with our faults, failures, lack of capacity, education, popularity and qualifications. Consequently, we carry a rather dim view of our ability to rise to the occasion and accomplish something spectacular. So we often fear to do what we want or what we believe is right and necessary because we have mistakenly presumed that it will be met with failure.

We are more impressed by what we think we can't do than what we might be able to accomplish if we would just try.

Sitting here twenty one or two years later, I am not disappointed in the life I have lived since then, nor the ministry I have conducted in these intervening years. However, it would certainly be interesting to know what that path would have brought us to had I chosen to rise to the occasion and accept it, and what God could have done in the city of Atlanta through it. This is by no means a justification for my decision, but I am personally acquainted with far too many men who did answer the call and now find themselves still broken and bleeding from the effort. Christians seem to have a penchant for violently chewing up and spitting out those who lead them, and the enemy that hunts them is none to kind either.

Chapter Six

Here's Yet Another Element of Fear

The arrangement of the system of the world, which is the system set up by satan to capture the hearts and minds of all its adherents, requires that you believe in the absolute efficacy of the system so that you will not only faithfully practice it, but teach others to do so as well – it's that discipleship thing. It is the performance thing, which is founded in fear, and if you buy into it then it holds all the promises you could ever dream of for acceptance and the validation of your personal value. It is just what you've always wanted. It has its own unique rewards, pay for play, and its own punishments for not abiding by its rules and honoring its guiding principles.

However, there's a much darker element that accompanies it which we don't realize is actually an un-advertised participant within the system. Its goal is to wreck the possibility of you fulfilling the purpose for your life by getting you to disqualify yourself through the application of the teaching of the system of the enemy. The strategy is the unconscious reinforcement or validation of an idea or a belief through similar repeated circumstances.

For instance, if I am happily strolling down the street on a bright sunny Spring day with a fresh breeze in my face and suddenly trip and fall down, dropping my coffee and my phone in a vain attempt to catch myself, I will likely say something offhanded like "clumsy oaf" with no other intent other than "pick up your feet and pay more attention to where you're stepping." Notice that there was no declaration of "You so-and-so" spoken, just a simple acknowledgement of an embarrassing, less than graceful act.

Over the next few weeks it happens again. A couple of weeks later you stumble and drop four cups of coffee you were bringing to your workmates, only this time you accuse yourself of being clumsy, with a few other choice words thrown in for emphasis. You even begin to joke about it by saying, 'I can't even walk and chew gum at the same time.'

What you have just done is to officially label yourself as being "clumsy" even though in each case you may well have been walking over rough ground and on old sidewalks that have been pushed up by large tree roots growing under them, augmented by zero maintenance attention. You assessment is that it was still your fault that it happened.

Congratulations! This new revelation has now become *your truth* by virtue of your keen observation of a few similar experiences. It may well not be *THE truth* because in fact, you are the most accomplished dancer in town, but alas, it is now *your truth*. And of course, ladies and gentlemen, your conclusion is backed up by iron-clad scientific methodology accepted the world wide: one postulates something by observing the results of multiple experiments conducted in a controlled environment. (We're golden! Except, possibly, the "controlled environments" part. But … hey, this is life.)

In religious terms, that's called a stronghold.

Your new truth builds the validity behind specific fears in much the same way all your other beliefs are changed to accommodate this new information: about who you are, what your limitations are, what your sensitivities are, how clumsy you are, how awkward you are in social situations, you can't tell jokes, everyone talks over you so no one ever listens to you, on and on. What becomes your normal response to these beliefs is about what you can't do, or who you are not?

In a very short period of time, you will automatically begin to compensate for what you believe (and fear) by avoiding those situations as best you can. When you are caught off guard in the midst of one of these situations your fear rises to gigantic proportions and you freeze, unable to respond in any intelligent way ... boom! Your worst fears are realized. First thing you know, you have reduced your social obligations to zero, and before long you have become totally isolated. Next thing you know, you're living in a cardboard box under a bridge somewhere. My, how the mighty have fallen! (and it was totally an inside job.)

What actually happened? Your personal belief system, based on your declarations about what you cannot do and who you cannot be, begins to actually prophesy a new reality for you and you will begin to see all of life through those skewed lenses. You will begin to draw exactly what you do not want.

The exact same thing happens for those who have always believed they'll be wealthy. They automatically look for opportunities to grow wealth and they invariably find them. But when you believe you will always struggle financially, in spite of what you know you want, you will never see the opportunities as opportunities, you will only be able to see them as risks ... all because of your fear-based beliefs. That's called cognitive dissonance – the inability to believe the message of another reality because you are fixed in the one you have settled on. You might be saying to yourself, "that sounds like the mantra of the Power of Positive Thinking" people, and you would be right. In order to think positively, you have to deal with the fears that created your negative thinking. In other words, you gotta Renew Your Mind. (Romans 12:2)

Fear is;

Fear is like an infant. It never remains that way for long.

Fear is never content to remain in the same neighborhood. It grows like cudzu till it affects every aspect of your life.

Fear will cause you to second-guess every decision you make.

Fear is not content to minister to you all by itself, so it will invite all its companions.

Fear will cause you to attempt to live life out of your head rather than your heart. You will now have to figure everything out.

Fear will kill spontaneity, so you'll have to stay in your current life, doing what you've always done.

Fear will not let you live in peace, for there is always something to address that may be sneaking up on you trying to catch you unaware.

Fear kills risk, and without risk there is no reward.

Fear makes you a prisoner inside your own self-devised 'safe' box.

Fear will make you question every voice, even God's.

Chapter Seven

There are even Sexual Implications

When we were created by God we were specifically and very intentionally created as sexual creatures; first of all, to aid in the procreation process, and secondly to experience the depth of relationship between man and woman.

Sex is the single activity that God designed to involve the whole being; spirit, soul and body. It is the height of expression of physical intimacy, combined with emotional feeling and spiritual connection. They are all part of sex. Little else affords this level of powerfully satisfying elements.

Sexual release activates some of the most powerful and addictive chemicals the human body can produce. The desire to experience those chemically induced experiences again and again unfortunately get connected with love and the apprehension of true relationship – the ultimate elixir.

We were created for relationship and created for love, and to experience the depth of it. Performance and perfectionism, which is founded in the fear of rejection, shuts down the emotional receptors which are key to fulfilling relationships. We want to be close to people so that we can feel accepted and often our need for love and acceptance leads us into sexual activity in the pursuit of it because we believe that is a natural expression of it. Our performance orientation informs us that we are able to throw ourselves whole heartedly into sexual participation on the promise that if we throw more of ourselves into it we'll get more out of what we think we need from it. The problem is that sooner or later we come to the realization that we're not actually getting the level of true love and acceptance that we had hoped to experience – our expectation becomes unrealized. When that doesn't materialize at the level we expect, disappointment appears and we conclude that this person is not "the one" for me because we fear that they will never be able to meet my deepest need. We will then begin the search for another partner, not realizing that we have fallen into the trap of the enemy.

When the ultimate experience of sex, in the context of relationship, becomes idealized, or perhaps the level of relationship that sexual activity implies becomes gets put on a pedestal, problems arise. When anything becomes idealized (or is seen as the solution to our fears, now defined as needs) its achievement gets put into a category all by itself – "the perfect union," thereby insuring dissatisfaction. When the pinnacle, the idealized version of sexualized love meets reality, whether it is a single event or the cumulative experience of decades of experiences, disappointment is inevitable. Relationships often fail and it's not the fault of sex at all, although it is often cited as the heart of the breakup, it is the idealization of relationship through sex that is the culprit, all because of our penchant to look at things through the eyes of performance and perfectionism.

You have to understand that fear (the reason for performance and perfectionism) is anti-relationship, and once adopted it will find its way into every area of your life. It will even join you in the bedroom.

Chapter Eight

The Misery of Fear

"We suffer more often in imagination than in reality."
Seneca the Younger (4 BC – 65 AD)

I am not sure that there is a great need to continue to try to convince you that any place you have agreed with fear in your life is bad, and that a major change in the way you think about yourself is needed to turn the ship around, but the following are a number of Bible verses that re-emphasize the misery that we inflict upon ourselves when we partner with fear on any level. As I said, it never remains small, like a cancer it always grows.

> Deuteronomy 28:66 *"And your life shall hang in doubt before you; and you shall fear day and night, and shall have no assurance of your life:"*
>
> Deuteronomy 28:67 *"In the morning you will say, Would God it were evening! and at evening you shall say, Would God it were morning! for the fear of your heart with which you shall fear, and for the sight of your eyes with which you shall see."*
>
> Job 4:14 *"Fear **came upon me**, and trembling, which made all my bones to shake."*
>
> Isaiah 21:4 *"My heart panted, fearfulness affrighted me: the night of my pleasure has he turned into fear to me."*
>
> Jeremiah 51:46 *"And lest your heart faint, and you fear for the rumor that shall be heard in the land; a rumor shall*

both come one year, and after that in another year shall come a rumor, and violence in the land, ruler against ruler."

Hebrews 2:15 *"And deliver them who through fear of death were all their lifetime subject to bondage."*

It is informative to note that fear alights simply through the prospect of the loss of life, whether it is real or imagined, death or dismemberment presumed to be waiting out in the street, the loss of a livelihood, a status in life or a way of life, a rumor or a troublesome edict. It's the favorite ploy of the enemy that is both the easiest to use and his most effective weapon.

Chapter Nine

An Unrealized Fear

My wife Pat and I have been involved in member care for a couple of missionary sending organizations for several years now and in the process have seen young people encounter fear from a quarter they never expected.

This encounter is from the perspective of the review of values that pertains to fear that you and I have seldom become introduced to, much less acquainted with. When young missionaries feel called to minister in a foreign country they have to leave everything they have known, including all their belongings, and in order to be effective, learn a new language and immerse themselves in a totally new culture. After about a year in their newly adopted country, they will usually head "home" again around the holidays for a brief sabbatical. They will try to catch up with friends, family and relatives, go to the mall, catch a couple of parties and do all the comfortable and familiar things they can't do in their "other home."

What happens is very predictable. They begin to catch up on all that they have missed, the weddings they weren't part of, the child births, eat mom's cooking, sleep in "their" bed, watch a football game or two, hear stories of graduation parties they couldn't attend, of road trips they missed out on, talk to friends who are starting exciting careers, etc, and they will begin to wonder if real life isn't actually passing them by because all these things were part of the dreams they had for their lives as they were growing up. Then the fear tinged questions begin to arise; How can I meet the man/woman of my dreams where I am and doing what I'm doing? Can I even see myself doing this where I am five years from now? Did I really hear God or did I just fall for the romantic idea of traveling to some exotic land to be part of a noble cause?

Fear comes in all shapes and sizes. It's not a one-size-fits-all sorta thing.

The result is that these 20-something missionaries will go back to their mission field for about three to six more months then decide they're done with the missionary life because they fear they will be missing out on "real life" as though what they were living wasn't it. It is the unresolved conflict of an old identity established by childhood memories and re-imagined dreams, validated by what they see their friends doing, versus a new life that is still very early in the process of formation.

The problem for missionary (foreign or domestic) workers is that it is much like gardening. It takes time to properly prepare the soil, plant the seeds, water and keep the competition of the weeds at bay until the plant gets big enough to grow on its own. The fruit may still be months or years away, or as in the case of most missionary work one may not actually be able to see the true fruit of your labors until it begins to appear in the next generation. That's a minimum of 25 years.

Consider also the fact that it takes a minimum of two years of consistent study to become proficient enough in a foreign language and culture before one can become relationally effective in the reason they came.

Whether these kids were aware of that dynamic before they signed up is unknown to me, but it has to be obvious that each of them is going to be faced with a similar decision: Can I deal with the fear of giving up a life that I know (and all my friends are currently joyfully experiencing) in exchange for one that has no guarantees at all? Can I truly believe and rely on God to open the doors to a life here that is preferable to the one I dreamed of back in the States?

> 2Thessalonians 1:13b " ... *God has chosen you for salvation through sanctification by the Spirit and through belief in the truth."*

The above verse has given rise to a great deal of understanding of the Christian life of late. From my previous Baptist background the idea of salvation was totally dependent upon a decision and a confession of faith in Jesus the Christ. This verse makes it plain that there's a bit more to it, in fact, it declares that there are two things that are needful in order to obtain salvation; continuous engagement in the "sanctification process and believing and appropriately applying truth to our lives.

It is obvious, at least to me, that we never grow, change in a positive direction, or learn anything outside of difficulty. Navigating the issues of life hand-in-hand with Holy Spirit teaches us a lot about who we are, what we are capable of and the power of the Holy Spirit to bring us through it all. Such is the essence of the sanctification process. We have to engage a multitude of challenging situations in life in order to be faced with our dysfunctional beliefs and the anti-relational postures and responses that have contributed to the damage the bumps in the road have initiated.

The thought that we have been "chosen" to walk this path to salvation is encouraging to me because Jesus said in John 15:16

that *"You didn't choose me. I chose you and appointed you to bear much fruit and that this fruit would remain."* That declares to me that there is both purpose (salvation) and fruit (results of sanctification) prepared for my life that requires His companionship to complete and His periodic intervention to insure that the train remains on the track and reaches its destination. Further, it says that I have been chosen to know and walk in the fruit of truth in my life (knowledge, understanding, wisdom and good decisions). I'm up for that!

Chapter Ten

What Does the Bible Say?

Deuteronomy 3:22 *"Ye shall not fear them: for the LORD your God he shall fight for you."*

Deuteronomy 31:6 *"Be strong and of a good courage, fear not, nor be afraid of them: for the LORD thy God, he it is that doth go with thee; he will not fail thee, nor forsake thee."*

Deuteronomy 31:8 *"And the LORD, he it is that doth go before thee; he will be with thee, he will not fail thee, neither forsake thee: fear not, neither be dismayed."*

Joshua 10:25 *"And Joshua said unto them, Fear not, nor be dismayed, be strong and of good courage: for thus shall the LORD do to all your enemies against whom ye fight."*

2Kings 6:16 *"And he answered, Fear not: for they that be with us are more than they that be with them."*

Psalms 23:4 *"Yea, though I walk through the valley of the shadow of death, I will fear no evil: for thou art with me; thy rod and thy staff they comfort me."*

Psalms 27:1 *A Psalm of David.* *"The LORD is my light and my salvation; whom shall I fear? the LORD is the strength of my life; of whom shall I be afraid?"*

Psalms 27:3 *"Though an host should encamp against me, my heart shall not fear: though war should rise against me, in this will I be confident."*

Isaiah 35:4 *"Say to them that are of a fearful heart, Be strong, fear not: behold, your God will come with* vengeance, even God with a recompence; he will come and save you."

Isaiah 41:10 *"Fear not; for I am with thee: be not dismayed; for I am thy God: I will strengthen thee; yea, I will help thee; yea, I will uphold thee with the right hand of my righteousness."*

Isaiah 44:8 *"Fear not, neither be afraid: have not I told thee from that time, and have declared it? you are even my witnesses. Is there a God beside me? yea, there is no God; I know not any."*

Isaiah 51:7 *"Hearken unto me, ye that know righteousness, the people in whose heart is my law; fear ye not the reproach of men, neither be ye afraid of their revilings."*

Isaiah 54:4 *"Fear not; for you shall not be ashamed: neither be confounded; for you shall not be put to shame: for you shall forget the shame of your youth, and shall not remember the reproach of your widowhood any more."*

Isaiah 54:14a *"In righteousness shall you be established: you shall be far from oppression; for you shall not fear:"*

Isaiah 59:19 *"So shall they fear the name of the LORD from the west, and his glory from the rising of the sun. When the enemy shall come in like a flood, the Spirit of the LORD shall lift up a standard against him."*

Romans 8:15 *"For you have not received the spirit of bondage again to fear; but you have received the Spirit of adoption, whereby we cry, Abba, Father."*

2Timothy 1:7 *"For God hath not given us the spirit of fear; but of power, and of love, and of a sound mind."*

1John 4:18 *There is no fear in love; but perfect love casts out fear: because fear hath torment. He that fears is not made perfect in love."*

Obviously, the Bible has a great deal more to say about God delivering us from the sources of our fear than about the ravages of fear itself and yet, it is there and described in rather graphic terms. Suffice it to say that fear has torment in it and all through it, which is precisely why the enemy brings it. It is a specific strategy of the enemy to rob you of whatever level of peace and sense of security that you have managed to attain. Since he hates God, he also hates you because God created you for His purposes and His glory and will do all in his power to make you as miserable as he can in an attempt to get back as God.

The good news is that the devil is limited in what he can actually do. If you remember, when Lucifer was thrown out of heaven (Luke 10:18) only one third of the angels rebelled and were given the left foot of fellowship along with him. That means that the good guys out-number the bad guys two to one. Then there's what Jesus did to the rest of the crew;

> John 12:31 *"Now is the judgment of this world; now will the **ruler of this world be cast out**."*

Jesus tells his disciples that as he dies, is buried and is resurrected the devil (satan) will no longer roam the earth himself bringing death and destruction. He (the devil) must now rule his dominion from a distance.

> Colossians 2:15 *"And having spoiled principalities and powers, he made a show of them openly, triumphing over them in it."*

The order of ruling demonic entities were stripped (spoiled, relieved) of their weapons and they are listed as follows; Death (the last enemy, 1 Corinthians 15:26 and 56), Thrones, Dominions, Principalities, Powers, rulers of the darkness of this world, spiritual wickedness in high places. Basically, Jesus stripped the vast majority of the weapons from the dark spiritual entities that touch earth, so that we can deal with them in the mighty name of Jesus.

Principally the primary weapons left to the enemy are fear and deceit. Both of which he is very good at using since he's had 6 or 7,000 years of experience dealing with mortals.

Since demons can't produce other demons as humans reproduce themselves, the enemy (satan) has had to rely on a unique strategy in an attempt to maintain his hold on this world. He needed to create a system that was self perpetuating rather than relying upon his demonic cadre to do all the work with each human appearing on the face of the earth. So, he created a system of thought that is founded in fear, since fear can be perpetuated. If you bought into the framework of the system then you became the victim of his system and you would begin to teach your children and your children's children its ways. We know the system as performance and perfectionism; the art of doing good things for a personal reward. If you follow the rules of the enemy's system it rewards you at first to get you to buy into it deeper and deeper, until eventually you become its slave.

We primarily recognize this fundamental element of this system as fear of death (or rejection.) Nobody I know ever embraced death willingly, except perhaps for those who chose suicide because their physical or emotional pain was too great to continue dealing with. The principal reason was that there was no assurance of what was on the other side. No one ever returned from the other side of death with video or pictures, or to document for us what it was actually like.

That's also part of the system of the world; you have to figure everything out through the strength of your mind alone. The system also prescribes that one can't rely on the Bible or blind faith in anything. If there is no concrete, scientifically backed, incontrovertible evidence that there is another dimension we enter into after life on earth, then it doesn't exist – it's just the product of someone's fertile imagination hoping for something better than what they have now.

Essentially, the system of the world is a demand to live life totally out of your head, rather than through your heart. Because failure is a definite possibility (just look at current marriage statistics), one must maintain the arduous process of examining every element of life for its ability to produce pain, harm or rejection (failure.) To make the job a bit easier, we are encouraged by the system to begin to catalogue everything; things that make me look good, things that I'm good at, things I don't do well at, situations where I struggle, people I don't do well with, things I can't handle and even a category for stuff I can't quantify.

The bottom line is that I don't want to be rejected, so I need to minimize the risks of that happening at work, in relationships, in athletics, in artistic expressions and even recreational activities, accompanied by all the practiced mental and conversational gymnastics, one can muster. One must stay at the top of their game – always on and ready to deal with circumstances that have a potential for failure in or around them.

This obviously that takes a lot of emotional energy and as a human we humans tend to make mistakes when we let our guard down, or get distracted. We can't always keep all the balls in the air, and all the plates spinning. Since many folks have spent so much time trying to avoid failure there was little or no time left for adopting strategies for relational problem solving, rescuing a career or emotional disaster recovery. When such a train wreck occurs, and it happens at some point in every life, the only options immediately open are fight, flight or freeze; perhaps passable as a survival strategy when caught out in the woods by yourself being threatened by crazed yak, but not all that appropriate when a fellow employee is making a spectacle of your newly acquired dance moves at the company Christmas party.

You see, the system of the world is built to pull you in and temporarily reward you for giving it your allegiance, and painfully punish you if you fail to live up to its exacting standards. It is absolutely unforgiving. Let me give you an example. The common remedy for significant emotional pain is self medication, whether it is food (Obesity is common, serious and costly. The prevalence of obesity was 39.8% and affected about 93.3 million of U.S. adults in 2015-2016.), television, sex, alcohol (Prevalence of Binge Drinking and Heavy Alcohol Use: In 2015, 26.9 percent of people ages 18 or older reported that they engaged in binge drinking in the past month.), exercise, adrenaline producing activities, twinkies, pot or hard drugs. These are the normal medications for all manner of pain and we recognize it all around us.

However, the last two on that list are not socially acceptable and the discovery of their use will quickly draw judgment from even those who tend to overlook almost anything. You know that if you run into someone who is a health food and exercise junkie that has lost more than 30 pounds you will probably come face-to-face with someone who has no tolerance for anything other than what they're doing, and they'll let you know that "their way" is THE way.

You see, the reasoning of the system of this world is that, *"If I do right, everything will be right."* There is just enough truth in that statement that you'll buy the whole enchilada. But anyone who has been around the block once or twice will tell you otherwise. Crap happens even to the best people we know! And seemingly for the craziest reasons. Let me give you perfect example; My father was a godly man, a hard worker, became wealthy by some standards, a perennial deacon in every Baptist church we were a part of, ministered in the local jail weekly, even walked a couple of miles a day. He died of cancer at 70. His sister however, was a chain-smoking chimney for 60+ years, she never exercised, ate horribly, drank the cheapest rot-gut whiskey money could buy for decades and outlived my dad by 20 years. She died from complications following a broken hip which occurred because she wouldn't ask for help getting off the toilet in a hospital. Go figure.

We have been taught by every institution we have ever been a part of that, *"If I do right, everything will be right."* That includes every school you've attended, every team you played on, every club you joined, every church you were a member of, and every company you ever worked for … and it includes your family of origin. Each of those organizations, at each phase of your life, sowed the seeds of performance and watered them carefully and religiously. Each of them made sure you followed all the rules, each with its own particular set of rewards and punishments. Society even has endearing sayings and terms it uses for those who play by its rules; the A-listers, the cream always rises to the top, the elite All-stars, etc., as well as for those who don't, or won't.

It is also one of the major reasons why we tend to root for the underdog. We fear being called a loser for it implies that there is something wrong with us because we didn't win, and likewise we hate to see those whom the experts have pre-determined to be the loser actually come up short. We would much rather have the likeable underdog pull one out of the hat and prove all the know-it-all prognosticators dead wrong. It keeps alive the hope that this could be our story. To make the contrast more poignant, the system even idolizes the worst to first seasons in every sport for the same reason: If you do right, it will be right." The inference is; if you do right, you'll win … all the time.

I find it interesting that as successful as the New England Patriots football team has been over the last decade that when it came time to face the Philadelphia Eagles in Super Bowl 52 the odds makers were in favor of New England, but the majority of fans outside of New England were for the underdog Eagles. We really want their story to be everyman's story, as well as ours, no matter who is arrayed against us, no matter the odds maker's calculations, we have a chance to win. I believe God made us that way – competitors to the end.

And it's all driven by fear.

Another reason for our propensity to embrace the ministry of fear is the intimate knowledge we have of ourselves and the historically chronicled list of failures and shortcomings we meticulously maintain, with which we are all too familiar for we live with them every day. No one wants to make the same mistakes over and over again, we do learn from them. Our memory is that good. However, the system of the world teaches us to be very cautious before we jump into something we've never done before and part of that cautionary process is to rehearse all the mistakes and unfortunate outcomes we have had to live through the consequences of as though each of them is a now a renewed potential outcome.

There is actually another aspect of the world's belief system, *"If I do right, everything will be right"* for the corollary then is also true, *"If I do wrong, everything will be wrong."* Note that it doesn't say, *"everything will go wrong"* because that would give us a possible way out. We can blame what went wrong on all kinds of stuff and people will buy it because they too have had stuff go south for no apparent reason. What it did say was that everything 'will go' wrong, that then is a direct reflection on us. That declares that we are a hopeless failure for whom there is no remedy. And we will work like h-e-double hockey sticks to keep anyone from saying that to us or about us.

Even the annals of world history endlessly laud the winners and provide mere footnotes regarding the losers. The reason is simple. **Winning is the reward for doing things right. Losing is the punishment for doing something wrong, or worse, being wrong.**

Let that statement sink in for a moment. When I have chosen to establish my personal value by doing things "right," I am immediately stripped of all value when I make a mistake or do something that in my eyes that is deemed to be wrong – I become wrong. That immediately creates an internal conflict that demands to be addressed because the pain that it generates cannot be ignored. Herein is the hellish part ... if the system of the world was what established my value, then it is the only one that can restore it. That, ladies and gentlemen, is the gerbil wheel from hell.

So a major part of rooting out fear from your life is a thorough examination of your value system. You have to know who you are where your motivations come from.

Chapter Eleven

The Command

If you will note in Matthew 24:6,

> *"And you will hear of wars and rumors of wars. See that you are not alarmed (in fear), for this must take place, but the end is not yet."*

In every verse we previously noted there is a command inherent in the promises of protection offered by God, *"Do not fear."* That means there is a command not to fall into fear regardless of the circumstances. Matthew 24:6 says, '*make a point to not be afraid, in spite of the news*.' That is something that we must voluntarily do. That doesn't mean that there will not be numerous opportunities for you to be afraid of what might happen. Nor does it mean that seeing the potential for disaster you shouldn't be prudent and make preparations for it. Denial never profited anyone.

The instruction for us is to not give into fear whenever the opportunity arises, with the implication that we have a choice to do otherwise. He never says, "don't do this!" without the possibility of us actually being able to do it. And rest assured, opportunities will arise to fear! If you don't create them, then the enemy will. The reward for not giving into fear is found in Isaiah 54:14, *"you shall be far from oppression."* (Oppression is exactly what the enemy has planned to dump on you.)   In other words, when you chose not to fear, *"No weapon formed against you will prosper."* (Isaiah 54:17) Both statements are not only true, but are an amazing statement of fact, if indeed you will choose not to fear – and you do have a choice.

Chapter Twelve

The Choice

Okay, let me review ... I understand that how I currently think and how I have responded in the past to opportunities to fear have created problems for me. I also understand that the failures that I have experienced in dealing with fear have conditioned me to always expect to encounter threatening circumstances and bad news, to which I will respond incorrectly again and walk away defeated and demoralized. And I know that every time I get backed into a corner, this is what happens. I have repeatedly responded to things by going immediately to fear, again and again.

And further, I understand that over time, my inappropriate responses to the stimuli of fear have caused me to re-order portions of my life to accommodate fear, which is now being reinforced by certain mindsets and habit patterns that I need to change ... but the problem is ... I still fear those things. I don't know how not to fear them. What can I do now?

Great question and part of the answer to it resides in the statement, "I still fear those things." One cannot simply deny fear after one has conditioned themselves to respond to it for years. It must be dealt with ruthlessly.

As you know, we have three hard-wired human responses to fear: fight, flight or freeze. Now I have heard individuals who are supposed to be learned men declare that these are the responses of primitive man and are the same responses of animals who have no reasoning skills or capacity, as though instantaneous reasoning was possible in life threatening situations. Sound great, but it was likely created by some isolated ivy league college professor whose only struggle in life was to find a convenient parking space at Starbucks.

God created us with that specific array of instinctual reactions to fear. In order to deal with our fears, I have to know what they are.

A few years back, a fellow that I admire and follow by the name of Arthur Burk , related this experience. He said the Lord had been trying to press in on the fear in his life, so he started praying this prayer, "Lord, where have I re-ordered my life to accommodate fear." Well, I thought that was a brilliant ideal so I decided to do it as well. I was not at all prepared for what I saw. It seemed that it was everywhere I turned. It was surprising because I have never considered myself to be a fearful person – I will admit that I hate heights and that I am none too fond of snakes, but otherwise I tend to keep my cool in difficult circumstances.

However, what that prayer began to reveal were a number of things that I had noticed previously but had no motivation to resolve. One of them was my reticence to return phone calls. I was forcing myself to do it, and it was uncomfortable, but I reasoned that you just have to suck it up and do what you have to do. It turned out that there was a shred of fear that the call was going to present a problem to me that I had no answer for. Now that sounds like a simple problem to negotiate because, after all, we are humans and can't possibly be expected to have the answer to every possible problem people face. And you would be right, except that that is not the expectation that I had created for myself.

It seems that fear has an uncanny way of weaseling its way into the various crevices of our lives virtually undetected. And in the process it has been able to convince us that our penchant for questioning things isn't fear, but is actually walking in wisdom. When the Lord shines His light on the issues it brings great clarity with it.

In order to make the process of change to living a life devoid of fear a bit easier I feel that is it helpful to sit down and divide our responses to fear into those three categories because, at least initially, the subject is a bit too big and complex to easily find a convenient handle to it. Some might find it a bit odd to look at it this way for even though we have three possible responses to fear, the circumstance in which fear presents itself tends to dictate how we respond. One of the reasons why I find that this is helpful is that in this situation, knowledge is power. One cannot fight effectively if we don't know what he/she is fighting.

For instance, if I am walking down the street and a random passerby suddenly whips out a large knife and comes at me, with what I assume to be an intent to kill me, I am automatically going to defend myself. However, if I am at a party and another attendee finds out that I am of anther political persuasion than he/she and begins to attack me verbally, the physical fight response is obviously not the correct choice, but I may choose to fight nonetheless, except it will be verbally.

In the first instance, I am not even presented with a choice in how I could or should respond or even why I should respond in that manner. If I am to survive I have to do something and my response will virtually be automatic. However, in the second instance I do have a choice, even though my past responses may have also been automatic. In fact, I still have any one of three choices. It is the motivation triggered by the specific circumstance that is behind the automated response that will reveal the lie I believe about myself and my personal value.

So here's the question to ask … Lord, in what situations do I automatically (freeze, flee or flight) and why? Where did I learn it and who or what taught it to me?

Obviously, none of us have the intent of going out and intentionally getting into an altercation as a means of investigating our inner most motivations. Believe me, your memory is quite helpful, and Holy Spirit will gladly fill in the any gaps for if needed. But half the battle is making up your mind to divorce yourself from fear. Without first having made the choice nothing else happens.

Here's the process as written by Martha Buford, a counselor, nurse and pastor in Sutherland Springs, Texas;

"Maybe you think it's too hard, you're too tired. You've tried and failed too many times.
Well, today is a new day, an opportunity waiting.
Doesn't matter if it's a new habit, a change in thought pattern, exercise, a new venture, a business ….
The First step is to decide to try again.
The next step is to show up.
Prepare, focus and go for it.
If you do not succeed, try again."

Chapter Thirteen

Investigate Your Current Beliefs

One of the first steps in almost any process is always Investigation. First you have to define what your fears are that have driven performance or self protection. It's time to do some introspection and discovery and to put some accurate names and definitions on the things you fear. Putting a name on what you fear is often an easy way of removing its power over you. Generally, the enemy is tried to install pushbuttons or triggers that will automatically cause the same dysfunctional response in spite of the fact that we fear different things for different reasons.

For many people this is a tough task because they have lived in denial of their emotions and only a couple of buckets to put what they know into: fear, anger, and blah (nothing.) To the extent that living in some level of fear is your issue, then you are going to have do some work, which will consist of not getting panicked when you feel something uncomfortable emotionally, but to stop and see if you can identify what it is you are feeling and put as accurate a name of it as you can. If you can't name what you are feeling then it's easy to get confused. For Anger and frustration may have the same general feeling, but frustration is only a subset of anger, or a harbinger of it and is generally not sufficient by itself as a trigger for aberrant behavior.

The next thing you will need to do is to stop and see if you can identify what triggered that particular emotion. Now I say stop, because what normally happens is gift in to the swell of emotion it brings, rather than pause briefly to see what it is. If you can do that, it will help you build an accurate definition for the emotion. It may only be a one-word thought. But that thought is the key to the motivation and the lie you believe about yourself. If emotional self-awareness is something you have had trouble with, by preferring instead to walk away and live in denial, this is going to be a difficult exercise for you, and it will take some time to get proficient at it. But a short deep breath followed by a pause can be all you need to make the determination.

> *Do not be conformed to this world, but be transformed by the renewal of your mind, that by testing you may discern what is the will of God, what is good and acceptable and perfect." Romans 12:2 (ESV)*

Now I hope you noticed the last line in the verse above because it states that there is a process involved in renewing our habit patterns when it comes to dealing with anything and particularly where fear is the issue. It is a progressive thing that requires staying with what we've begun. When you were little you didn't learn to run immediately. It started with crawling, walking, toddling, then finally to running that involved falling down a number of times. This is no different.

One thing you can count on is the Lord's help in this process because, as He said, *"It was for freedom that Christ set us free."*

Figuring out exactly what you fear is the beginning of freedom.

One thing to beware of is the enemy as well, as some of your less mature, well-meaning friends who are also would-be psychologists, would love to make postulations and helpful suggestions as why you think that, or the root of this lie is this or that, blah, blah blah. I have encountered several cases where people have suggested that the source of someone's fear, pain and dysfunctional responses were caused by being molested as a child and they don't remember it because those memories are too deeply repressed. Immediately dismiss such suggestions for they will only confuse things and lengthen the process for you. The enemy loves to get things out of sequence. It's one of his favor strategies.

If indeed that is at the bottom of one or more of your fears, there will be a time when it's appropriate to deal with it. Someone's wild guess is not sufficient evidence to launch off into trying to resolve it.

Purpose

Now I can't leave this section without speaking to your life purpose because it is obviously integral to your belief system, and its fulfillment is also integral to enjoying life. Then too, as I've said before, "If you don't know where you are going, any road will take you there." Aimlessly wandering through life is a recipe for misery. We were created to live life intentionally in pursuit or, or in accord with the accomplishment of our purpose.

In the Jeremiah, Chapter 1 we read,

> 4 *Now the word of the LORD came to me, saying,*
> 5 *"Before I formed you in the womb I knew you, and before you were born I consecrated you; I appointed you a prophet to the nations."*

I believe that these two verses are a declaration of how the Lord created each of us. He created us for a specific purpose even as He did for Jeremiah and He did before you were born. The only difference was that Jeremiah pursued the Lord and He told him what that purpose was. Interestingly, being set apart and appointed for that job as we read above is exactly what God does with us because there a things you are drawn to and other s you are repulsed by. Being drawn (even curious or keenly interested) to something is the same as being set apart to do it. Further, when you are "appointed" to do something it is your desire to do, but someone else must make it happen, eg. make the appointment to the office or the job. In other words, the purpose for which you were created for God insured that he poured everything into you that you would need to: first, be interested in it, second, desire to prepare for it and thirdly, seek to enter into it. The God enters the picture again to bestow favor upon you so people will see your value and then open doors so that you can engage in it meaningfully.

The key is that typically people have believed a number of lies about themselves that causes them to disqualify themselves for entering or achieving the purpose God has for them. If you will faithfully discover those lie and choose to deal with them, you will find purpose and expression for your life.

Chapter Fourteen

Document Your Current Beliefs

The next step is Documentation. After you have defined what you actually fear, there is power in acknowledging fears in several different ways. The first thing is ownership. If you know you have this or that fear, and don't want whatever it is, after it is named and defined it then more easily becomes your choice either to keep it or throw it away. It loses much of its power to continue to hold you.

Without personal ownership of the issue there is no responsibility for its resolution.

You will then need to write these fears down on paper. Often this simple process provides us the time to consider them from another angle: what you have actually been afraid of and when examined, how small it really is. One of the companions of fear is always intimidation, which tries to make problems look bigger and more imposing than they really are. Writing it down allows us to indelibly etch on our conscious mind note only a reinforcement of the need to dispose of it, which is also part of the process of creating exercises to help us actualize our desire, but puts individual fear in proper perspective. They are not as insurmountable as you have always presumed, and when brought out into the light, none of them are as big and scary as they were before.

After you have written down on paper all your fears, being as specific as you can, make a copy of it and save it for the next step. Take your original out-doors somewhere and declare (out loud and in a loud voice) over them that you are divorcing them – this dance is done, you are not continuing it and any place of agreement between you is broken and any implied contract between you, regardless of whether it was ratified by your action of inaction, is now officially canceled, and the terms of it are now null and void. Then destroy it: burn it, shred it, throw it in the trash, whatever. Make a statement! Even make a little ceremony of it to mark the occasion.

At some point in this process the enemy is going to start to realize that if we don't do something this dance really will be done, so there will be an attempt on the part of the enemy to regain the lost ground and re-establish the foothold that it is losing. So expect some retaliation. It's not going to be very big, but it will be noticeable. So lean into the lord for strength and realize that when this happens victory is right around the corner.

Chapter Fifteen

Declare Your New Life

The next thing you need to do is Declare what you are going to do now that your divorce from fear if final. Your voice is a powerfully creative tool. Since you and I were made in God's image we have been given several of the very same characteristics that He has. If you recall, the book of Genesis documents the creation story. In the process of creating everything we can see and touch God "spoke" it all into existence. His heart determined what He wanted to create, what each element looked like in its finished form, complete with all of its characteristics and each with its individual purpose for being created, as well as, how it interacted with everything else in the universe – then His voice determined what was created by what it uttered. His spoken words created everything our five senses engage, except humans.

So in order to fulfill your purpose on earth, the very reason God created you, you are going to have to start acting like you were created by Him and do what He does.

Now the point of this, which you need to grasp with both hands, is this; if you do not speak what you want it can never be created in this realm. Neither Holy Spirit, nor a single angel, is ever activated to do one blessed thing with your unspoken thoughts. Nothing happens. But when you speak what you want to happen, it will do no good to speak it as – an "I wish" or an "I want." It must be spoken (phrased) as though it is a finished work – a confident affirmative statement of what you envision in its completed state. Then the angels are activated to begin the process of bringing it to pass. Suddenly the encouragement to change offered by friends, relatives and strangers is there where it never existed before. The Holy Spirit begins to help with creative strategies to alter your thinking and begins to show you positive things about yourself that you never realized before. Suddenly you are drawing resources, seeing support appear where it didn't exist before, experiencing favor in surprising ways.

But perhaps one of the coolest things about declarations is that once you declare what the finished work (big clue) will look like when all the dust has settled on this new arrangement, you will have created the framework for a new reality for yourself. That new reality begins to reset the order of your life and provides you with the focus necessary to work consistently to meet your new goals. That new reality also provides borders for you to operate within that help insure that new habits are built along the way. It also provides a new higher standard against which all previous responses to fear are measured. That provides you with more Holy Spirit assisted self control to do what you want rather that what was previously automatic and unfruitful.

As powerful as declarations are, in the final analysis they are nothing more than vain imaginations and ways to blow more time and resources that produce nothing if they are not given the Good-Housekeeping-Seal-of-Approval by God himself. If you remember the verse in Proverbs 16:9,

> "The heart of man plans his way, but the LORD establishes his steps."

If we take our plans to the Lord in advance of launching out into them on our own, He will help us not only modify them to ones that will succeed, but He will actually partner with us in the execution o f them. That's a good thing, because He's never failed once at getting what He want done.

Chapter Sixteen

Renewing Your Mind

The next step is Renewing the Mind. As we have given fear room to hang out in our thought processes we were unaware that these fears were actually based in lies. In the middle of every trauma, every emotionally charged event, the enemy comes to feed you a lie. It is always the same: a lie about you, a lie about God and a lie about those involved in whatever happened.

The process for renewing your mind begins with the discovery of the lies that you believe about yourself. A great many people are well aware of a couple of them because they've been in the back of their mind for decades – that small voice that says, "I can't lean this" or "I won't remember that" or my personal favorite, "I'd better not try that because I'll fail doing it and I can't have that!"

At other times we have to rely on God to show them to you because they are so intertwined with the way you see and process things that you are totally unaware of the wrong way you view issues. This why King David prayed this simple, yet profound prayer asking the Lord to uncover the hidden motivations and funky belief systems he had founded his life upon,

> "Search me, O God, and know my heart! Try me and know my thoughts!
> 24 And see if there be any grievous way in me, and lead me in the way everlasting! Psalms 139:23-24 (ESV)

You see, in many cases we cannot address the things we can neither see or don't understand because the misconceptions we are working under that shape how we conduct our lives and relationships are all we've ever known and I naturally assume that that's the way everybody else sees them as well. In order to live our lives as we were created we have to live in complete truth, not a half-truth, and the world we live in has worked very hard to corrupt the truth and keep you from living from it.

There is always a segment of the population, and we've met quite a few lately, who are so emotionally shut down that they are totally unaware of the lies they believe. They have chosen to reason their way through every problem and when there's a blockage they either try to ignore it or distract themselves with something "more important" to stay busy so they don't have to think about it. (That's emotional 'flight" driving the bus.) Self-awareness is the only way out of this hole.

I had the experience of introducing a young artist acquaintance of mine to another acquaintance of mine who runs an art gallery. As the artist began the introduce the work she brought, she began to give a litany of all the troubles she had had in the industry going back fifteen years, most of which had little or nothing to do with why she was there or what products she was selling. Now, in her defense, it was an exploratory introduction, but the decidedly negative viewpoint of herself deeply colored everything she said. The pieces she brought in to view were amazing works of art and any of his customers would have been proud to have anyone of these items grace their homes.

The difficulty for this woman was that she, like so many others, was totally unaware of how she came across and how it perfectly portrayed how and what she thought of herself. It was not healthy and I was embarrassed for her because she has a lot going for her that she obviously has no capacity to appreciate.

Building awareness of how you speak about yourself is one of the key elements needed in the discovery of what lies you believe about yourself specifically, and you can only do that by paying attention to how you feel during such times and asking yourself why you feel that way. If you choose to ask that question, wait for an answer. Your own voice will tell you. If that's hard for you, ask a friend to tell you how you come across to others when you are forced to talk about yourself.

Now, I'm not talking about the arrogant horse behinds who will gladly talk about themselves at the drop of a hat. I am speaking to those of you who think: "I am needy. I don't belong here. Everyone else is superior to me. This is uncomfortable because someone may refute me. I have no qualifications to stand in this place because everyone here is smarter and knows more than me."

As I said before, you know most of the lies already. Sit down and ask yourself, "Do I remember any situations in the past where I consciously recoiled from or shied away from doing what I needed to do because something within me said," I can't do this? Taking a test, learning to do something new, asking someone out on a date, or engaging in a contest." Any, or all of these could be one of the hints that you believe a lie that you are not enough. You need to know what that is. Remember, the Bible says,

> "*For as he thinketh in his heart, **so is he***:" Proverbs 23:7 (KJV)

Chapter Seventeen

Write Down The Truth

The next step is writing down the exact opposite of the lies you have bought. You can choose to use Biblical truth, what God says about you, or you can counter every lie you wrote down with its logical opposite. If you have believed the lie or thought you were dumb, then write down, " I am smart. I am a quick leaner and can master any subject." If you have believed the lie that you are never enough and you will always lose in anything you put your hand to, write this down (or something like it that better fits your particular belief), "I will succeed in anything I try. I am smart enough, perceptive enough, creative enough, even convincing enough to do what is necessary to be and remain successful into anything I attempt." If you are working on something specific right now, plug that in. The key is that you must describe the opposite of the lie you have believed in a manner that says it is already completed and has years of experience already behind it. The reason behind this it is that in declaring things in this manner formulates and established your personal vision for a preferable future and puts positive language to it. Here's another verse to ponder,

> "Where there is no vision, the people perish:" Proverbs 29:18 (KJV)

Now what this is says is that you and I must have goals. We were created to be bold and to take risks in life; things that that we are willing to sacrifice force for, work for, plan for, pray for and invest in. If you do not have a firm vision, or none at all, then circumstance will guide you because you have no pre-determined direction and the lies you believe about who you are and what you are capable of will cripple your efforts along whatever path you have chosen. Because of the effectiveness of those embedded lies you will always second guess your choices, then the following question will always arise, "What if I get it wrong?" God has already has an answer for that too.

> *"The heart of man plans his way, but the LORD establishes his steps."* Proverbs 16:9

In other words, you can plot your course and head off in that direction. However, if that path or proposed destination is not going to be a blessing to you, or it will put you in a place you are not supposed to be, then if you have given the whole thing to the Lord, and are sensitive to his redirection, He will redirect your steps to get you on the right course (path) that will take you to the destination you are supposed to arrive at. If you are not remotely interested in His help then you will miss all the clues and attempts at redirection He is providing.

Early on in my life I didn't know any of this, nor was I particularly interested in His direction because I thought it was all up to me. – and this is true, we all have a free will (personal choice) that God will honor. I am not blaming this on my Southern Baptist roots and a lack of instruction in this area, but either no one taught it anywhere I was, or I wasn't paying attention. Consequently, when the Russians beat America into space, John F. Kennedy made a plea for young people to engage in the sciences and mathematics. So I went off to college and studied electrical engineering. After college I went to work for an architectural/engineering consulting firm in

Houston, TX. After the new wore off, I quickly came to realize that I didn't like engineering much at all. After almost four years I made a career move.

The next fifteen years were actually directed by circumstances, that is, the need to make a living and support a family. Stuck in there was a year long stint with a Christian ministry where all manner of spiritual doors for practical training and preparation for ministry began to open. The Lord used business to get us to Colorado for that introduction and education. I returned to engineering to make a living but doing personal ministry nights and weekends characterized the next ten as a result of that introduction. That turned into a ten year long season of preparation. So the route to ministry for me seemed somewhat circuitous, but the destination the Lord had in mind all along was finally attained.

Was all that a waste of time? That's probably the way a victim mindset would view it. It was certainly full of life lessons that I would have been just as satisfied to learn another, less painful way. Nonetheless, I am just grateful that my ship finally made landfall at a wonderful port. Could I have acquired the appropriate vision for my life and avoided all those changes and bumps in the road? Let me answer it this way. Unless we intentionally choose to seek the Lord for the answer to that question, and at the same time look to the clues provided by self-awareness, then we are left pretty much up to our own devices. In that situation we are simply hoping to make the right decisions. However, at any point along the journey you can choose to let Him be the guide, or at least seriously consult Him in your decision making process, consequently, you can expect Him to straighten out your crooked path.

Is what I am doing now, something I would have considered before college? I don't think so because I had never crossed paths with anyone who was a either a secular counselor, or a prayer minister. In fact, I didn't even run into a full-time prayer minister until I was 42, so I had no earthly idea such an animal existed. When I did finally encounter one he was reasonably wealthy and retired, so that was the only model I had even then. And ... had I known how little one makes in this profession trying to get started in it, I would probably have avoided it like the plague. At age 42 we were still raising kids, so we probably wouldn't have considered ut to be a viable option either.

So what was the point of all that? If you don't know where you are going, any road will take you there, and many of those destinations you don't want to visit because it takes you longer to leave them than you can possibly imagine.

Personal vision, as well as freedom, is not a luxury. It is an absolute necessity and you create it with verbal expressions of your mouth that are soon embraced by your heart. So sit down and write out the best view of who you are and what you intend to do with the balance of your life, and create this new reality with the spoken declarations of your mouth. It however, must be founded on the truth about you and what you are capable of that strongly counters all the lies you have believed.

Chapter Eighteen

Fear versus Healing

Here's another aspect of fear that as a Christian you need to consider;

Check out the passage located in Mark 2:1-12. The friends of a paralytic find Jesus speaking in someone's home and bring him there so Jesus could heal him. The crowd was so large they couldn't get near him, so they came up with plan B. Let's tear a hole in this guy's roof and let him down right in front of Jesus. Jesus' response was interesting to me because of two things seen in verse 5, "*And Jesus seeing their faith said to the paralytic, 'Son, your sins are forgiven.'*" Then a minute or two later after addressing the temple scribes, He says to the man, "*Take up your bed and walk.*" The paralytic picked up his stretcher and walked out. Presumably he helped with the restoration of the roof.

The healing experienced by the paralytic was apparently some combination of three things; the faith of his buddies recognized by Jesus, the forgiveness pronounced for the sins of the paralytic, which was somehow responsible for him becoming paralyzed, and the verbal pronouncement of healing by Jesus.

So what do we know? The faith of the paralytic's friends provided the opportunity for him to be healed; proximity to Jesus was absolutely necessary. And so it is for us today. In contrast to the above situation, the woman with an issue of blood for twelve years was in a similar situation in Mark 8:43-48 and in her effort to be healed she had to defy cultural taboos (break through a barrier) in order to get close to the person of Jesus. Jesus said that it was her faith that made her whole, in spite of the fact that there was no interaction between the two prior to her healing.

The same was true for the infirm man (of 38 years) at the pool of Bethesda (John 5:1-14) who came into contact with Jesus and was the recipient of a drive-by healing. His faith was actually more directed to the periodic presence of a healing angel that stirred the water at the pool. Nonetheless, Jesus pronounced again, *"Take up your bed a walk."* Then in verse 14 Jesus says, *"Sin no more, that nothing worse may happen to you."*

However, the healing of the paralytic in Mark 2 had another wrinkle in it that is particularly interesting to me; the forgiveness of sin that was required for this particular healing. As is typical for many Bible stories we are not given all the particulars about the condition of this man's paralysis, specifically its origin. It may have been something a congenital defect, or something that went wrong during the birthing process. It may have been due to a subsequent disease, or an accident at some point in his life. No matter what the origin of his paralysis was, what we do know is that he had good friends, which says that he was obviously relationally influential in his limited community. People without position, authority or influence in a community normally would not have such a cadre of determined individuals at their side. Those fellows were apparently sufficiently determined to improve his condition that the idea of tearing the roof off a stranger's house to lower their friend in through it didn't require much consideration.

There are a couple of other such instances in Jesus' ministry, but each stand in stark contrast to the bulk of his healing which came as an act of faith on the part of the supplicant, or was a pointed demonstration of the Kingdom of God. The disciples of Jesus acknowledged in John 9:2 the prevailing belief of the religious system of the day was that the result of sin was understood to be disease, or a major physical handicap, or in this guy's case blindness. See also John 5:14 where Jesus tells the healed invalid to *"Sin no more, that nothing worse may happen to you."* again linking the consequences of personal sin to some dire physical issue.

My wife and I operated a healing room for seven years in North Carolina and it became common knowledge that approximately 85% of the physical issues that people suffered with were the result of an emotional or spiritual issue.

The process we went through to assist in obtaining healing for someone that came in for prayer involved a process of having the client repent of sins they committed, or renouncing the lies they believed, breaking generational curses, etc. Sometimes it was effective. At other times it was not. The healing of the paralytic recounted in Mark 2 Jesus employed none of those tactics. He simply did what He told his disciples to do in He followed that up with, *"If you forgive the sins of any, they are forgiven them; if you withhold forgiveness from any, it is withheld."* John 20:23 (ESV)

Remember this in the context of what was just stated, *"… as he (Jesus) is, so are we in this world."* I John 4:17 (KJV) The obvious understanding that we need to walk away with is this … although there are occasions when someone must repent and turn away from sin that is destroying them in order for God to be able to heal them, it is ultimately the legal position of the enemy that has been used to afflict them that must be overturned. Pronouncing forgiveness for sin is your Jesus-given right and responsibility, and all that is needed to overturn the enemy's case and usher in healing. We still have to pronounce healing, just as Jesus did in the vast majority of cases.

So why do we chose not to take that road? I have a couple of suggestions;

1. Our faith is not well developed and we don't want it tested.
2. Our lack of discernment in these situations is a key factor.
3. The faith for healing of the one the before us in most cases is non-existent. So essentially we want to operate on their faith rather than ours. That way if nothing happens it's their fault.
4. We that find solving the cause-and-effect relationship between sin and sickness to be more appealing than standing in authority.
5. And there are always those who want to be healed because it interferes with the stupid stuff they are doing. They don't really want to change, they just want to feel better, so we tend to leave them in their ignorance suffering the consequences of their actions as though they deserved it.

However, for a clearer understanding of our responsibility to deal with fear in our lives we need to take a look at the entire passage surrounding 1 John 4:17.

> 1John 4:16-20 " *And we have known and believed the love that God hath to us. God is love; and he that dwells in love dwells in God, and God in him.*
> *17 Herein is our love made perfect, that we may have boldness in the day of judgment: because as he is, so are we in this world.*
> *18 There is no fear in love; but perfect love casts out fear: because fear hath torment. He that fears is not made perfect in love.*

19 We love him, because he first loved us.
20 If a man say, I love God, and hate his brother, he is a
liar: for he that love not his brother whom he hath seen,
how can he love God whom he hath not seen?" (KJV)

The biggest reasons for not engaging the physical issues people have with healing are principally these two; 1) we don't really love people regardless of their issues, or the cause of them, and 2) we fear that we'll be embarrassed if we pronounce healing and nothing happens. In other words, we love our own lives more than expressing compassion for others through pronouncing healing. Comparatively speaking, we effectively hate others because we love our safe lives more. To protect our fragile egos we turn to what we choose to call healing prayer, asking God to heal a person suffering from a physical malady. By doing so we dump the responsibility for healing totally upon God, so when nothing happens it's God's issue not ours. We justify our lack of action by saying that we honestly don't have the power to heal anyone of our own volition (Acts 3:12) so it is appropriate that the responsibility fall on God, totally denying the example of faith demonstrated by the paralytic's friends.

> *"Truly, truly, I say to you, unless a grain of wheat falls into the earth and dies, it remains alone; but if it dies, it bears much fruit. 25 Whoever loves his life loses it, and whoever hates his life in this world will keep it for eternal life."* John 12:24-25 (ESV)

This is a choice left to each of us. Deal with your fear or lose your life. Choosing to live with fear is like choosing to sleep with the enemy rather than becoming a friend of God. Check out verse 15 below.

Hebrews 2:14 'Since therefore the children share in flesh and blood, he himself likewise partook of the same things, that through death he might destroy the one who has the power of death, that is, the devil,
15 <u>and deliver all those who through fear of death were subject to lifelong slavery."</u>

Chapter Nineteen

Intentionally Face Your Fears

One of the reasons unrecognized fear wreaks so much havoc is because fear is often the symptom of a much bigger problem: missing maturity. Lacking maturity means we are not fully grown and developed for our age and stage of life. Something in our character is underdeveloped that needs to be cultivated. Missing maturity happens because of good things that are missing or because bad things happen that should not happen. The Life Model calls this Type A and Type B traumas.

Scripture says the earth cannot bear the strain of this hidden iceberg in people who are given great responsibility and authority. Putting unprepared, immature individuals in positions of authority to manage power and prosperity is intolerable, even catastrophic.

While our brain is wired for self-preservation, of which fear is the urgent response to fight, flee or freeze from a threat, fear is good for about 90 seconds before something needs to change. Staying stuck in fear can be toxic to our health and disruptive to our relationships. Many disorders and much detriment happens to our body and mind when processing breaks down in the brain's emotional control center.

Since you have spent valuable time investigating your fears, naming them and searching with the Lord for the source of them, you have a vey good idea of how and when they trigger responses that are out of proportion to the stimulus or create dysfunction.

Now is a good time to create a plan to face each of those in turn. Obviously, if you have a quasi-irrational fear of poisonous snakes there is no need to force yourself into a dangerous confrontation with them, however there is a need to master that which is attempting to master you. Go to a zoo and watch them through a glass wall. Take note of your responses and ask the Lord to show you what you need to do or say to deal with this irrational fear. Do it and don't leave the area until you no longer feel the tension of the fear.

The same would be true in dealing with a fear of heights. There is no need to go to the roof of a tall building and force yourself to lean far out over the edge. Taking a few trips up and down in the glass enclosed elevator of a fancy hotel might be in order. Unless you do something to face the fear itself and find that it actually has no power over you, it always will.

This applies equally to all manner of fears and phobias; public speaking, meeting new people, entering contests, dancing in front of strangers, wearing edgy garments, dyeing your hair, eating weird food, in short, doing something you've never done before.

Chapter Twenty

Courage

Some time ago I was sitting before the Lord and this is what I asked, "Speak to me about fear."

His response was,
"I would rather speak to you about courage.

It is curious to humans that I would do this because they have all deemed fear to be their greatest enemy. You are fully aware that the enemies of mankind have used it terrorize, bully and manipulate people to get their way since the dawn of time. You certainly respect its presence when there is a project that is blocked or progress is frozen. You blame it for all manner of human maladies including manifestations of numerous human illnesses – and rightly so – and yet to me, fear is simply the absence of courage.

I have created man with a free will and the ability to choose; right or wrong, good or bad, to give or hold onto things, to fight or flee, to love or to hate, and so on. But as my Word says, I did not create you with fear.(2Timothy 1:7) I created you with courage, but you chose to learn fear instead. It has robbed mankind of many of the blessings that I have put in the earth for man's benefit.

Courage is actually your birthright. Its presence in you produces hope. It is why people are longing for affirmation, for prophetic words and why they turn to fortune tellers. They want to be reminded of the good things they are capable of; the things that lie before them and connect with the slivers of hope within them that their future will be brighter than they perceive their present to be. Those words build a measure of hope, which leads to declarations, which produces a mild confidence, which will eventually activate the courage I put in them, which in turn will cause them to attempt to engage that which was prophesied.

But the fact remains that this is the process of coming out of fear into courage, a process that I gave you because I did not create you with fear. I created you to be courageous."

The phrase, "Be of good courage" appears 30 times in the Bible in the King James Version. That's three (the number of the God head) times ten, the number of God's order, the way things are supposed to be.

The words "Fear Not" appear 144 times in the Bible. That's twelve time twelve. Twelve is the number of God's government and twelve squared is to remind us that we need to re-align ourselves to His proper order, government and purpose – the way things were created to be.

The word "Fear" appears 385 times in the Bible, more than one for every day of the year. Sometime regarding fear (KJV) of the Lord,, or respect of the potential for the collateral damage that occurs by being around things that God has declared to be dangerous, but often as the source that paralyzes motivation.

"I have given humans a choice – all of them –to be courageous in the face of fear in order that they might be able to do that which is both in My heart and in theirs.

What are you fearful of?

Why?

What is the worst thing that could happen if your worst fears were realized?"

Look at;

Psalms 138:8 *"The Lord will be fulfill His purpose for me."*

What do I need to be afraid of?

" If God be for me, who can be against me?" Romans 8:31

"You shall be far from terror, for you shall not fear." Isaiah 54:14

"You are not terrified by your adversary, which to them is proof of their destruction, and your salvation." Philippians 1:28

"Fear is a reaction. Courage is a decision." Winston Churchill